THE GREATNESS OF
THE GREAT COMMISSION

Other books by Kenneth L. Gentry, Jr.

The Christian Case Against Abortion, 1982, rev. 1989
The Charismatic Gift of Prophecy, 1986, rev. 1989
The Christian and Alcoholic Beverages, 1986, rev. 1989
The Beast of Revelation, 1989, rev. 1993
House Divided: The Break-Up of Dispensational Theology (with Greg
    L. Bahnsen), 1989
The Greatness of the Great Commission, 1990, 1993
He Shall Have Dominion: A Postmillennial Eschatology, 1992
Lord of the Saved: Getting to the Heart of the Lordship Debate, 1992
*God's Law in the Modern World: The Continuing Relevance of Old
    Testament Law*, 1993

THE GREATNESS OF
THE GREAT COMMISSION
The Christian Enterprise in a Fallen World

Kenneth L. Gentry, Jr.

Institute for Christian Economics
Tyler, Texas

Library of Congress Cataloging-in-Publication Data

Gentry, Kenneth L.
   The greatness of the Great Commission : the Christian enterprise
in a fallen world / Kenneth L. Gentry, Jr.
     p.   cm.
   Includes bibliographical references and index.
   ISBN 0-930464-50-8 (pbk.) : $9.95 (alk. paper)
   1. Great Commission (Bible). 2. Evangelistic work -- Philosophy.
3. Dominion theology. 4. Fundamentalism -- Controversial literature.
5. Dispensationalism -- Controversial literature. 6. Millennialism.
7. Sociology, Christian. I. Title.
BV2074.G45 1990   90-15500
269--dc20   CIP
                                          r90

Institute for Christian Economics
P. O. Box 8000
Tyler, TX 75711

To my covenant children:

Amanda, Paul, and **Stephen**

As "the heritage of the Lord," they are
"like arrows in the hand" (Psalm 127:3, 4).

TABLE OF CONTENTS

PUBLISHER'S FOREWORD

Gary North

So God created man in his own image, in the image of God created he him; male and female created he them. And God blessed them, and God said unto them, Be fruitful, and multiply, and replenish the earth, and subdue it: and have dominion over the fish of the sea, and over the fowl of the air, and over every living thing that moveth upon the earth (Gen. 1:27-28).

And Jesus came and spake unto them, saying, All power is given unto me in heaven and in earth. Go ye therefore, and teach all nations, baptizing them in the name of the Father, and of the Son, and of the Holy Ghost: Teaching them to observe all things whatsoever I have commanded you: and, lo, I am with you alway, even unto the end of the world. Amen (Matt. 28:18-20).

There is a tremendous need today for evangelism. By this, I do not mean simply the limited personal evangelism of tract-passing. In any case, the tract is no longer with us. The newsletter and the cable channel TV interview show have replaced tracts. What is needed today is a comprehensive program of worldwide evangelism that brings the message of salvation to every individual on earth, in every walk of life.

Having brought people into the kingdom of God through conversion, God then asks them to begin to make a difference in their world. He does not mean that they should spend day and night passing out tracts or the equivalent thereof; He means that they should reform their lives, their families, and their daily walk before Him and men. Evangelism means teaching people to obey God's law, through the empowering of

God's Holy Spirit. Evangelism means *obedience*. This is the message of Jesus: "If ye love me, keep my commandments" (John 14:15). He also said:

> He that hath my commandments, and keepeth them, he it is that loveth me: and he that loveth me shall be loved of my Father, and I will love him, and will manifest myself to him (John 14:21).

This is not the ethical message of modern fundamentalism. Fundamentalism's ethical message is the opposite: "No creed but the Bible, no law but love!" Fundamentalism's cultural message is that Christians have nothing specifiic to say to a dying world except to tell individuals to get ready to be pulled out of it, either at the Rapture or at death (preferably the former, of course, since fundamentalists really do expect to get out of life alive). They intend to leave nothing behind. *They plan to disinherit the future.* Best-selling dispensational author Dave Hunt says the pre-tribulational Rapture is so much better than dying:

> (1) If we are in a right relationship with Christ, we can genuinely look forward to the Rapture. Yet no one (not even Christ in the Garden) looks forward to death. The joyful prospect of the Rapture will attract our thoughts while the distasteful prospect of death is something we may try to forget about, thus making it less effective in our daily lives.
> (2) While the Rapture is similar to death in that both serve to end one's earthly life, the Rapture does something else as well: it signals the climax of history and opens the curtain upon its final drama. It thus ends, in a way that death does not, all human stake in continuing earthly developments, such as the lives of the children left behind, the growth of or the dispersion of the fortune accumulated, the protection of one's reputation, the success of whatever earthly causes one has espoused, and so forth.[1]

I call this *scorched-earth evangelism*. It warns Christians that the Great Tribulation will destroy the Church's legacy after the Rapture. It will disinherit the gospel. But this is not what God teaches. Christians have their assignment: *to conquer in His name*.

---

1. Dave Hunt, "Looking for that Blessed Hope," *Omega Letter* (Feb. 1989), p. 14.

Biblical Evangelism

When God says to "evangelize," He means we should tell the good news to the world: not easy news, or inexpensive news, but good news. The good news is this: *Jesus Christ has overcome the world.* "Ye are of God, little children, and have overcome them: because greater is he that is in you, than he that is in the world" (I John 4:4). *The Great Commission is a great victory.*

Most fundamentalists want a watered-down gospel message suitable for children, and only for children. The problem is, children grow up. What do you tell a newly converted adult when he asks the question, "All right, I have accepted Jesus as my Lord and Savior. Now what do I do?" Modern fundamentalism says mainly all he has to do is tell someone else about what just happened to him. Then that person tells another, and so on, until the Rapture revokes the Great Commission.

Modern fundamentalism looks at the gospel as if it were some kind of gigantic chain letter scheme. Nothing is of value in God's sight except keeping this chain letter going. But the gospel is not a chain letter. It is the good news that Jesus has already overcome this world and gives His disciples authority to extend His dominion in history before He returns in judgment.

It is our job to demonstrate this victory in our lives, meaning every aspect of our lives. We should exercise dominion. We should do this as church members first, but in all other realms.

The Dominion Covenant

Had there not been a fall in Eden, every person would self-consciously define himself or herself in terms of dominion under God (Gen. 1:26-28). This was what God told man his task must be: to serve as God's intermediary over the earth. This assignment is called the cultural mandate by Dutch Calvinists in the tradition of Abraham Kuyper. I call it the dominion covenant.[2] The dominion covenant did not cease with Adam's fall; it was reconfirmed at the "new creation" after the Flood:

---

2. Gary North, *The Dominion Covenant: Genesis*, 2nd ed. (Tyler, Texas: Institute for Christian Economics, 1987).

And God blessed Noah and his sons, and said unto them, Be fruitful, and multiply, and replenish the earth. And the fear of you and the dread of you shall be upon every beast of the earth, and upon every fowl of the air, upon all that moveth upon the earth, and upon all the fishes of the sea; into your hand are they delivered. Every moving thing that liveth shall be meat for you; even as the green herb have I given you all things. But flesh with the life thereof, [which is] the blood thereof, shall ye not eat. And surely your blood of your lives will I require; at the hand of every beast will I require it, and at the hand of man; at the hand of every man's brother will I require the life of man (Gen. 9:1-5).

The Great Commission is necessary because man, in his rebellion against God, has forgotten Who it was who gave him his assignment. He has forgotten to Whom he is historically and eternally responsible. Men need regeneration in order to regain God's favor. Man is still under God's rule, but he refuses to acknowledge this fact. He worships other gods, either made by him or found in nature (Rom. 1:18-21). He may even worship nature itself (pantheism), personifying it as feminine.

The fact is, God's two assignments are linked together by their status as covenants. God issued the dominion covenant (family) first because man had not yet rebelled. He then issued the Great Commission (church) because He had established the judicial foundation for a New Covenant, a universal covenant that binds men of all races and backgrounds under God.

The Church and the Great Commission

The institutional Church is the primary administrator of the Great Commission, for it alone controls lawful access to the sacraments. The family is the primary covenantal agency through which the dominion covenant is to be extended. The family supports the local church financially in most cases, except when there is an emergency for a particular family. Churches are not equipped, as non-profit institutions, to initiate projects under the dominion covenant. The task of the local church is to preach, give moral guidance, heal the sick, feed the destitute, and administer the sacraments. It is not designed to innovate businesses and other dominion-oriented projects.

The State is not a primary covenantal agency in either of these tasks, evangelism or dominion, although it imitates both Church and family when it becomes autonomous and rebellious. The State is required by God to defend both Church and family from physical attack. It not to become an initiating agency. Its task is negative: to impose negative sanctions against evildoers (Rom. 13:3-7). Socialism is the result of a pseudo-family State; empire is the result of the pseudo-Church State.

We preach the centrality of the Church. But we also preach that there is a whole world to bring under God's righteous rule.

Escaping Responsibility

It is always difficult to sell personal responsibility. The dominion covenant establishes mankind's responsibility over the creation and under God: hierarchy. This inescapably hierarchical system of responsibility places some men over others in certain institutions and in certain circumstances: a bottom-up appeals court system. Certain men must exercise dominion over others, depending on what institution we are talking about.

Those who enjoy exercising power are not hesitant to misuse this inevitable hierarchical aspect of every society. They endorse the *power religion*. Those who fear responsibility are willing to endure oppression for the sake of security. They endorse the *escape religion*. What neither of these religions preaches is freedom under God, which means *self-government under God's Bible-revealed laws*. The God of the Bible brings predictable negative sanctions in history and sends people into eternal torment if they refuse to make a covenant with Him. This God is hated.

Christianity is the alternative to both the power religion and the escape religion.[3] It teaches the whole Bible, which includes the dominion covenant. It preaches restoration with God, meaning the restoration of man's law-governed authority over the whole world.[4] But without redemption, and without obedience to biblical law, men cannot be trusted by God to exercise

---

3. Gary North, *Moses and Pharaoh: Dominion Religion vs. Power Religion* (Tyler, Texas: Institute for Christian Economics, 1985), pp. 2-5.
4. Gary DeMar, *Ruler of the Nations* (Ft. Worth, Texas: Dominion Press, 1987).

lawful dominion. So, by grace, He has made a way of restoration. This is the saving, healing gospel of Jesus Christ. Nothing is to be excluded from Christ's healing: not the family, not the State, not business, not education, and surely not the institutional Church. Salvation is the salve that heals the wounds inflicted by sin: every type of wound from every type of sin.

This is why the Great Commission was given: to enable mankind to return to faithful service under God and over the creation. God's salvation brings us back to the original task: *to exercise dominion to the glory of God, in terms of His Bible-revealed law.* The gospel will succeed in history before God comes again to judge the world. The Bible gives us hope for the future.[5]

The Restoration of Hope

Rev. Gentry in 1981 wrote a superb essay with the same title as this book. It appeared in the Chalcedon Foundation's *Journal of Christian Reconstruction*, which I edited: the "Symposium on Evangelism." I realized at the time that his view of the Great Commission, if accepted widely by the Church, would transform not only the Church but the Christian concept of civilization. I asked him to write this book in 1990, which he did.

The book provides many of the footnotes and Bible references that he had to skip over in his original essay. This is a scholarly treatment of the subject, although it is eminently readable. It is comprehensive — so much so, that I do not expect pietistic Christians to reply to it. As I wrote in 1990, this book will silence them. So far, it has.

This book presents Christian activists with their God-given marching orders. In contrast, pietists of all eschatological views will continue to define God's kingdom narrowly enough to match their limited vision of the gospel's effects, and they will achieve successes of comparable magnitude.

The Greatness of the Great Commission is written as a motivational book for people who need to be persuaded. If you are willing to look at the sources listed in the footnotes, you are

---

5. Kenneth L. Gentry, Jr., *He Shall Have Dominion: A Postmillennial Eschatology* (Tyler, Texas: Institute for Christian Economics, 1992).

likely to rethink the whole question of both the scope and method of evangelism. Dr. Gentry has done his homework.

His critics owe it to God, to themselves, and to their followers to do at least an equal amount of homework. Merely insisting that Gentry has misunderstood the Great Commission is not the same as proving it. Disproving his thesis will take more than a two-page book review in some in-house magazine or journal.

It is my hope that this book will serve the Church well in a future era of historically unprecedented revival. Such a revival, if it comes in our day, will be international. I hope that it will also be comprehensive. Without a theological case for the comprehensive nature of God's redemption in history, there can be no sustained revival. This book provides the biblical evidence for the comprehensive nature of the Great Commission.

If Gentry is correct in his analysis of the meaning of the Great Commission, then every church, every seminary, and every parachurch ministry needs to re-examine what it is doing and why. Such re-examination will be painful, but not nearly so painful as the looming judgments of God in history — another doctrine that the modern Church has conveniently forgotten.[6]

There will be great resistance to his thesis within the modern Christian world. It is difficult to sell responsibility, and there is now so much to do. Our task today has grown so great because so much undone work has accumulated for so long. Christians have neglected their comprehensive assignment from God. We have lost at least three centuries, most of the churches, and every university. We can and must win back these institutions, plus many more that Christianity never controlled. We have been commissioned to do it. *We must get to work.*

Gentry in his books adopts gentle rhetoric, precise arguments, and many Bible verses. This book is no exception. His books are eloquent testimony against the oft-heard statement from this or that critic that "I can't accept theonomy because of North's harsh rhetoric and Bahnsen's theological intransigence." We must be careful to distinguish excuses from reasons.

---

6. Gary North, *Millennialism and Social Theory* (Tyler, Texas: Institute for Christian Economics, 1990), ch. 8.

INTRODUCTION

"All authority has been given to Me in heaven and on earth. Go therefore and make disciples of all the nations, baptizing them in the name of the Father and the Son and the Holy Spirit, teaching them to observe all that I commanded you; and lo, I am with you always, even to the end of the age" (Matthew 28:18b-20).

In these sixty-one words from Matthew's gospel we have what rightly has come to be known as "The Great Commission." This Commission was issued by our Lord Jesus Christ only a few days after His resurrection and not long before His ascension into heaven.

The Great Commission has long served, and still today continues to serve, as the marching orders for Christ's Church in the world.[1] Rare is the Missions Conference that has met without making reference to this text. Few are the denominations that have been established without some appeal to it. Most orthodox Christians from all denominational connections and from all theological perspectives have held this forth as their banner in the service of Christ.[2]

But is the Great Commission understood properly today? Is the fullness of its import comprehended by its adherents? Do we really grasp *The Greatness of the Great Commission?* These

---

1. Reference to this passage is found as early as Ignatius (A.D. 50-115), *Epistle to the Philadelphians* 9; Irenaeus (A.D. 130-202), *Against Heresies* 3:17:1; Tertullian (A.D. 160-220), *Prescription Against Heresies* 20.

2. I do recognize that there are some evangelicals, who do not understand the Great Commission as incumbent upon the Church. For more information on this unusual phenomenon, see: Chapter 12.

questions are becoming major issues in evangelical circles.

The Issue

Surely the most important debate between liberal and orthodox theologians today has to do with the issue of the *inerrancy*
of Scripture. Is the Bible God's Word and without error? Does
it possess impeccable authority as the certain revelation of God?
This is a fundamental issue with great implications for Christian
faith and practice.[3]

Among evangelical Christians today a related discussion has
developed. This discussion has to do with the problem of the
apparent *irrelevancy* of Scripture. Is the whole of Scripture
confidently to be applied to all of life today? Is God's Word
practical for Christian living and social conduct in every aspect
of modern society?[4] And the significance of the Great Commission lies at the very heart of this important discussion.

Basically, the issue of the greatness of the Great Commission
may be resolved by properly answering the following three
major questions.

1. *What Is the Great Commission?* A. Is the Great Commission
a wholly new divine program to respond to sin, which is set in
stark contrast to and is discontinuous from the Old Testament
program? B. Or is it the capstone of the longstanding covenantal program of God to respond to sin, and the fruition of the
development of the progress of redemption that is continuous
with the Old Testament?

2. *What Is the goal of the Great Commission?* A. Is its goal pessimistic, directing the Church bravely to be a witness in a hopelessly lost and dying world despite overwhelming resistance,
while "snatching brands from the fire"? B. Or is its goal opti-

---

3. See the following for helpful studies in this area: Rousas John Rushdoony, *Infalli-
bility: An Inescapable Concept* (Vallecito, CA: Ross House, 1978). James Montgomery Boice,
Does Inerrancy Matter? (Oakland, CA: International Council on Biblical Inerrancy, 1979).
Ronald Youngblood, ed., *Evangelicals and Inerrancy* (Nashville: Thomas Nelson, 1984).

4. See: Greg L. Bahnsen, *By This Standard: The Authority of God's Law Today* (Tyler,
TX: Institute for Christian Economics, 1985). Rousas John Rushdoony, *The Institutes of
Biblical Law*, 2 vols. (Vallecito, CA: Ross House, [1973], 1982). Gary North, *Tools of
Dominion: The Case Laws of Exodus* (Tyler, TX: Institute for Christian Economics, 1990).

mistic, empowering the Church successfully to promote the salvation of the world against all resistance, while leading the vast majority of men to salvation?

3. *What Is the nature of the Great Commission?* A. Is its nature individualistic, seeking the salvation of individual lost sinners, with a view to training them in their private walk and public worship? B. Or is its nature holistic, seeking the salvation of individual lost sinners, with a view to training them in their private walk, public worship, *and* the development of Christian culture?

The Approach

The three questions just presented touch on vitally important issues related to the Great Commission and the Christian enterprise in a sin-laden world. In this work I will seek to answer *from Scripture* these crucial questions. In doing this I hope to promote a better apprehension of the greatness of the Great Commission.

My approach to the Great Commission primarily will be to offer a focused and careful exegetical analysis of Matthew 28:18-20. I will also draw into consideration a broad array of biblical texts from throughout Scripture, in order to flesh out the full biblical meaning of the Commission. The issue before us is, as stated before, the *relevancy* of Scripture — *all* of Scripture — to modern life and culture.

It is my hope that this study will both enlighten and challenge: My design is to enlighten Christians to the teaching of Scripture on this crucial issue and to encourage them to apply biblical principles to all of life. The Commission before us is truly great, for it speaks of "*all* authority" (Matt. 28:18) to disciple "*all* nations" (Matt. 28:19), with a view to our teaching them "*all* things" (Matt. 28:20a) Jesus taught His disciples. It also holds out the certain hope that Jesus will be with us "*all* the days" (Matt. 28:20b) to see that it is done.

Before I begin in earnest, I must point out the foundations of the Great Commission. There are two ultimate foundation stones: creation and covenant. I deal with relevant matters drawn from creation and covenant in the first two chapters.

Part I
FOUNDATIONS

1

THE CREATION MANDATE AND
THE GREAT COMMISSION

Then God said, "Let Us make man in Our image, according to Our likeness; and let them rule over the fish of the sea and the birds of the sky and over the cattle and over all the earth, and over every creeping thing that creeps on the earth." And God created man in His own image, in the image of God He created him; male and female He created them. And God blessed them; and God said to them, "Be fruitful and multiply, and fill the earth, and subdue it; and rule over the fish of the sea and over the birds of the sky, and over every living thing that moves on the earth" (Gen. 1:26-28).

The Christian faith is concerned with the material world, the here and now. The Christian interest in the material here and now is evident in that: (1) God created the earth and man's body as material entities, and all "very good."[1] (2) Christ came in the flesh to redeem man.[2] (3) His Word directs us in how to live in the present, material world.[3] (4) God intends for us to remain on the earth for our fleshly sojourn, and does not remove us upon our being saved by His grace.[4] As is obvious from these four observations, we have a genuine concern with the here-and-now. Just as obvious is it that this concern is necessarily *in light of the spiritual realities mentioned*: God, redemp-

---

1. Gen. 1:1-31; 2:7.
2. Rom. 1:3; 9:5; 1 John 4:1-3.
3. Rom. 12:1-2; Eph. 5:15-17; 2 Tim. 3:16-17.
4. John 17:15; Job 14:5; 2 Cor. 5:9-10.

8 THE GREATNESS OF THE GREAT COMMISSION

tion, revelation, and providence.

At death, all men enter the spiritual world, the eternal realm (either heaven or hell).[5] But prior to our arrival in the eternal state, all men live before God in the material world,[6] which He has created for His own glory, as the place of man's habitation.[7] The Great Commission necessarily speaks both to the present state (by giving our duty in the material world) and to the eternal state (by showing the means of our entry into heaven). In other words, it speaks to issues regarding body and soul.

Both of the foundation stones for our study of the Great Commission are found in Genesis. In fact, the very foundations of all of reality, revelation, and redemption are laid in the book of Genesis, which makes that book of primary significance to the Christian faith. The very title "Genesis" is derived from the Greek translation[8] of Genesis 2:4a: "This is the book of the generation [Greek: *geneseos*] of heaven and earth."[9] The word *geneseos* means "origin, source."[10] And it is in the opening chapters of Genesis (chs. 1-3) that we find the essential elements of these foundational truths.

The Mandate Explained

The Creation Mandate was given at the very creation of the

5. 2 Cor. 5:8; Phil. 1:23: Luke 16:22-23. On the doctrine of hell, see: Gary North, *Heaven or Hell on Earth: The Sociology of Final Judgment* (forthcoming).
6. 2 Chr. 16:9; Psa. 33:13-15; Prov. 15:3; Acts 17:28; Heb. 4:13. No U. S. Supreme Court "right-to-privacy" decision can alter this truth.
7. Psa. 24:1; 115:16; Prov. 15:3; Dan. 5:23; Acts 25:24-31; Rev. 4:11.
8. The Greek translation of the Old Testament is called the Septuagint, and is often abbreviated: LXX (the Roman numeral for seventy [*sept*]). It is a translation of the original Hebrew, which was done in the second century B.C., supposedly by seventy (actually seventy-two) Jewish elders. See: the second century B.C. writing *Letter of Aristeas* and Augustine, *The City of God* 18:42. (Septuagint is almost always mispronounced; the proper pronunciation is to accent the first syllable, not the second: SEP-tu-a-jint.) The ancient Hebrew title for Genesis is *B'reshith*, which is the first word in Gen. 1:1 and is translated "in the beginning."
9. The term *geneseos* occurs frequently in Genesis as a heading to various sections. See: Gen. 5:1; 6:9; 10:1; 11:10; 11:27; 25:12; 25:19; 36:1; 36:9; 37:2.
10. The root of the Greek term (*gen*) is found in many English words, such as "genes," "generation," "genealogy," and even my own name, "Gentry," which means "a well born person." All of these English terms have something to do with beginnings.

earth and mankind upon it: on the sixth day of the creation week.[11] Consequently, the Mandate serves an important purpose in distinguishing man from the animal, plant, and protist kingdoms: only man is created in "the image of God" (Gen. 1:26; 9:6), a little lower than the angels (Psa. 8:5). One vital function of this image is that of man's exercising dominion over the earth and under God. As is evident in their close relation in Genesis 1:26, the *dominion drive* ("let them rule") is a key aspect of the *image of God* ("Let us make man in Our image") in man.

Thus, man has both a basic constitutional *urge* to dominion as a result of his being *created* in God's image and a fundamental *responsibility* to do so as a result of his being *commanded* in the Creation Mandate. Man's distinctive task in God's world in accordance with God's plan is to develop culture.[12] Culture may be defined as the sum deposit of the normative labors of man in the aggregate over time.[13] Adam was to "cultivate" the world (Gen. 1:26-28), beginning in Eden (Gen. 2:15).

Interestingly, early fallen man was driven to cultural exploits

---

11. Gen. 1:26, 31. That each of the six days of creation was a literal twenty-four day and not a day-age, as some neo-Darwinian Christians argue, is demanded by the following exegetical evidence: (1) "Day" is qualified by "evening and morning" (Gen. 1:5, 8, 13, 19, 23, 31), which specifically limits the time-frame. (2) The very same word "day" is used on the fourth day to define a time period that is governed by the sun, which must be a regular day (Gen. 1:14). (3) In the 119 instances of the Hebrew word "day" (*yom*) standing in conjunction with a numerical adjective (first, second, etc.) in the writings of Moses, it never means anything other than a literal day. Consistency would require that this structure must so function in Genesis 1 (Gen. 1:5, 8, 13, 19, 23, 31). (4) Exodus 20:9-11 patterns man's work week after God's original work week, which suggests the literality of the creation week. (5) In Exodus 20:11 the plural for the "days" of creation is used. In the 702 instances of the plural "days" in the Old Testament, it never means anything other than literal days. (6) Had Moses meant that God created the earth in six ages, he could have employed the more suitable Hebrew term *olam*.

12. See: Francis Nigel Lee, *Culture: Its Origin, Development, and Goal* (Cape May, NJ: Shelton College Press, 1967); Abraham Kuyper, *Lectures on Calvinism* (Grand Rapids: Wm. B. Eerdmans, [1898] 1961); Henry R. Van Til, *The Calvinistic Concept of Culture* (Philadelphia: Presbyterian and Reformed, 1959); Francis Schaeffer, *How Should We Then Live?: The Rise and Decline of Western Thought and Culture* (Old Tappen, NJ: Fleming H. Revell, 1976).

13. The first entry under "culture" in *OED* reads: "1. Worship; reverential homage." It also directs attention to the entry "cult," where the Latin *cultus* ("worship") is dealt with. The idea of "culture" is closely related to religious activity. *The Compact Edition of the Oxford English Dictionary*, 2 vols., (Oxford: Oxford University Press, 1971), 1:622.

well beyond the expectations of humanistic anthropologists and sociologists. We see the effect and significance of the Creation Mandate very early in history in the culture-building exploits of Adam's offspring. In the Bible, man is seen acting as a dominical creature, subduing the earth and developing culture, even despite the entry of sin. Man quickly developed various aspects of social culture: raising livestock, creating music, crafting tools from metal, and so forth (Gen. 4:20-22). In that man is a social creature (Gen. 2:8), his culture building includes the realm of political government, as well; this is evident in God's ordaining of governmental authority (Rom. 13:1-2). Upon his very creation, not only was man commanded to develop all of God's creation, but he actually began to do so. Culture is not an accidental aside to the historical order. Neither should it be to the Christian enterprise.

It is important to realize that the Cultural Mandate was *not* withdrawn with the entry of sin into the world. The mandate appears in several places in Scripture *after* the Fall: Genesis 9:1ff; Psalm 8; Hebrews 2:6-8. But the new factor of sin did necessitate divine intervention and the supplementation of the original Mandate with the new factor of *redemption*.

Immediately upon the fall of Adam into sin, God established the covenant of grace, which secured man's redemption. Genesis 3:15 promises the coming of a Redeemer ("the seed of the woman"), who will destroy Satan ("the seed of the serpent"). This verse is often called the "protoevangelium," or the "first promise of the gospel." The gospel of God's saving grace began at this point in history.[14]

And it is the Great Commission which comes in as the capstone of this proto-redemptive promise.

The Mandates Compared

There are a few evangelicals who disassociate the Creation (or Cultural) Mandate from the Great Commission,[15] which

---

14. Rom. 1:1-2; Gal. 3:8; Heb. 4:2 speak of the "gospel" in the Old Testament. God has always saved man by His grace, apart from works and based on the work of Jesus Christ.

15. See for example the recent works by Hal Lindsey, *The Road to Holocaust* (New

has also been called the New Creation (or Evangelistic) Mandate. This is an unfortunate mistake that detracts from the greatness of the Great Commission and a proper engagement of the Christian calling in the world. Nevertheless, the two mandates are intimately related. This may be seen from several considerations.

Both Mandates Are Granted at Strategic Times

In its setting, the Creation Mandate occurs as the "swelling of jubilant song" at the accomplishment of God's creative activity.[16] At that time, the creation had just been completed and pronounced "very good" (Gen. 1:31-2:2). Genesis declares that "God finished His work."[17] The Greek word for "finished" here is *suntetelesen*, which is based on the root word *teleo*. On the basis of the completion of God's work, the joyful declaration is given.

The New Creation Mandate, too, occurs at the climax of divine labor. It was given at the completion of Christ's work in securing man's redemption, not long after He declared, "It is finished" (John 19:30).[18] His statement in the Greek is *tetelestai*, which is based on the root word *teleo*, the same root found in the statement in Genesis 2:2.

Because of the work of Christ, a "new creation" has begun; there are several verses that speak of salvation as a new creation.[19] The old creation involves the material world in which we live; the new creation involves the spiritual world, which governs the life we live as saved creatures. Consequently, the old creation and new creation correspond to one another. Thus, the Creation Mandate and the New Creation mandate

---

York: Bantam, 1989), pp. 272ff.; Dave Hunt, *Whatever Happened to Heaven?* (Eugene, OR: Harvest House, 1988), pp. 225ff.; and H. Wayne House and Thomas D. Ice, *Dominion Theology: Blessing or Curse?* (Portland, OR: Multnomah, 1988), pp. 150ff.

16. C. F. Keil and Franz Delitzsch, *The Pentateuch* in *Commentary on the Old Testament* (Grand Rapids: Wm. B. Eerdmans, rep. 1975), 1:64.

17. Translation of the American Standard Version (1901) and the Revised Standard Version.

18. See also John 17:4; Heb. 1:3.

19. 2 Cor. 5:17; Gal. 6:15; Eph. 2:15; 4:24.

supplement each other, as well.

Both Mandates Claim the Same Authority

The ultimate authority of the Triune God specifically undergirds both the Creation and the New Creation Mandates. The Creation Mandate was given directly from the mouth of God, who had just created all reality by means of His spoken word (Gen. 1:26-31). This was the very God who said, "Let *Us* make man in *Our* image" (Gen. 1:26), thus indicating His Trinitarian being.

The activity of the later New Creation Mandate is to be performed "in the Name of the Father and of the Son and of the Holy Spirit," the Triune God (Matt. 28:19). It also was uttered by the very mouth of God: God the Son, who holds "all authority in heaven and earth" (Matt. 28:18) and by whom the universe was created.[20]

Both Mandates Are Given to Federal Heads

The Creation Mandate was initially under the federal headship of Adam. By "federal" is meant that Adam did not act just for himself, but for us. When he was tempted in the Garden of Eden (Gen. 2:16-17) and fell (Gen. 3:6ff), he did so in our stead, as our federal head (Rom. 5:14ff). We are all born sinners[21] on the basis of this federal connection with Adam. We do not earn our sinful estate; we are born into it.

The New Creation Mandate is under the continuing headship of the Last Adam, Christ.[22] When Christ lived according to God's Law through all His trials (Heb. 4:15) and died under that Law (Gal. 4:4), He did so in our behalf, as our federal head (Rom. 5:14ff). Christians are all born again[23] on the basis of this federal headship connection with Christ. We do not earn our righteous standing; we are born into it.

---

20. John 1:3, 10; 1 Cor. 8:6; Col. 1:16-17.
21. Gen. 8:21; Psa. 51:5; 58:3; John 3:6; Eph. 2:1-3.
22. 1 Cor. 15:45; Matt. 28:18, 20.
23. John 1:12-13; 3:3; Jms. 1:18; 1 Pet. 1:23.

Both Mandates Engage the Same Task

Both the Creation and New Creation Mandates are designed for the subduing of the earth to the glory of God. The Creation Mandate was to begin at Eden (Gen. 2:15) and gradually to extend throughout all the earth (Gen. 1:26-28). It was restated after the Great Flood (Gen. 9:1-7).

The New Creation Mandate, which supplements, undergirds, and restores man ethically to the righteous task of the Creation Mandate, was to begin at Jerusalem (Luke 24:47) and gradually to extend throughout the world (Matt. 28:19). As we will show in the following chapters, the Great Commission sets forth the divine obligation of the true, created nature of man. It seeks the salvation of the world, the bringing of the created order to submission to God's rule. This is to be performed under the active, sanctified agency of redeemed man, who has been renewed in the image of God.[24]

Both Mandates Were Originally Given to Small Groups

The Creation Mandate originally was given to Adam and Eve (Gen. 1:27), and then renewed to Noah and his sons (Gen. 9:1). The New Creation Mandate was given to Christ's disciples (Matt. 28:16) for all ages (Matt. 28:20).

It is clear from the New Testament that the few original disciples, though initially intimidated by the resistance to Christ from their native countrymen, eventually overcame their cowardly hesitance. Upon witnessing the resurrection of Christ, they became convinced of the power of God. They received the command to "disciple all nations" on the basis of "all authority in heaven and on earth." They accepted the obligation to preach the gospel to "every creature" (Mark 16:15).

Both Mandates Require the Same Enablement

As I have shown above, the Creation Mandate establishes a close connection between the interpretive revelation regarding man's being created in God's image (Gen. 1:26a, 27) and His

---

24. Col. 3:10; Eph. 4:24.

command to exercise rule over the creation order (Gen. 1:26b, 28). Man lives up to His creational purpose as He exercises righteous dominion in the earth. God has implanted within man the drive to dominion. The entrance of sin, however, perverted godly dominion into a desire to "be like God" (Gen. 3:5).

The New Creation Mandate provides the essential restoration of the image of God in knowledge, righteousness, and holiness (Eph. 4:24; Col. 3:10). The Creation Mandate is consequently undergirded by the restorational activity of God by means of the New Creation power.

Conclusion

A major foundation of the Great Commission is found firmly placed upon the bedrock of Scripture and creation in Genesis. An awareness of man's divinely ordained task in the world is essential to grasping the greatness of the Great Commission, as I will show more fully in the exposition of the Commission itself. The Great Commission is a corollary of the Creation Mandate.

But the second foundation stone, to which I alluded above, must now be considered. That foundational issue regards God's covenant with man.

2

THE COVENANT AND
THE GREAT COMMISSION

And in the same way He took the cup after they had eaten, saying, "This cup which is poured out for you is the new covenant in My blood" (Luke 22:20).

Structuring the God-ordained task of man in the world is a distinctive legal framework, which is abundantly exhibited in Scripture. That legal structure is known as "covenant." The Bible is very much a covenant document. Even a cursory reading of Scripture demonstrates the Bible has a strongly covenantal cast: the word "covenant" occurs almost 300 times in the Old Testament[1] and thirty times in the New Testament.[2]

The Covenant in Scripture

To understand the implications of the covenant idea and its foundational significance for the Great Commission's redemptive truth, we need a little background introduction.

Historical Background

Mutually established covenants were common among the ancients, examples of which are numerous both in Scripture

---

1. Sometimes the Hebrew word for "covenant" (*berith*) is translated either "confedera-cy" (Oba. 7) or "league" (Josh. 9:6ff; 2 Sam. 3:12ff).
2. In the King James Version New Testament the Greek word for "covenant" (*diatheke*) is sometimes rendered "covenant" and other times "testament."

and in ancient non-biblical texts. By way of example, we might notice the covenants between the following parties: Abraham and Abimelech (Gen. 21:22-32), Isaac and Abimelech (Gen. 26:26-31), Jacob and Laban (Gen. 31:43-55), Joshua and the Gibeonites (Josh 9:3-15), and Solomon and Hiram (1 Kgs. 5:12). There are many others.

Such mutually established covenants are similar to modern contracts and treaties, although with some important differences.[3] These human covenants were between roughly equal parties: man to man.

Also revealed in Scripture are the much more important sovereignly established divine covenants. The parties in these are decidedly unequal: the infinite God and finite man. Some of the divine covenants receiving emphasis in Scripture are those established with: Adam (Hos. 6:8), Noah (Gen. 6:18), Abraham (Gen. 15:18), Israel (Exo. 24:8), and David (Psa. 89:3). Off in the future from the Old Testament perspective lay the glorious, final "New Covenant" (Jer. 31:31-34). Paul summed up the various Old Testament covenants as being "the covenants [plural] of the promise [singular]" (Eph. 2:12). There is both a basic unity undergirding the divine covenants, as well as a progressive development in them.

Legal Definition

Succinctly stated, a covenant may be defined as:

> A solemnly established, legal oath-bond, which creates a favorable relation between two or more parties based on certain specified terms, and which promises blessings for faithful adherence to those terms, while threatening curses for unfaithful departure from them.[4]

Let us consider the basic qualifying elements of our defini-

---

3. Covenant and contract cannot be equated. See Gary North, *The Sinai Strategy. Economics and the Ten Commandments* (Tyler, TX: Institute for Christian Economics, 1986), pp. 65-70.

4. A helpful study of the covenant in Scripture is found in O. Palmer Robertson, *The Christ of the Covenants* (Phillipsburg, NJ: Presbyterian and Reformed, 1980).

tion.

A Covenant Is a Legal Oath-bond. In a covenant the parties solemnly swear to maintain the obligations outlined in the covenant contract. Of divine covenants, Scripture notes regarding God: "Since He could swear by no one greater, He swore by Himself" (Heb. 6:13). A covenant establishes a *legal* bond to which appeal can be made by either party, if the terms are breached. Thus, a covenant establishes and protects specified rights.

Furthermore, each party to the covenant was to have a copy of the covenant contract. This is why the covenantal Ten Commandments were on *two* tables of stone.[5] Each stone held a complete copy of the Ten Commandments for each party, God and man.[6]

A Covenant Establishes a Particular Relation. The purpose of a covenant is to establish a favorable relationship. The heart of God's "covenants of the promise" (Eph. 2:12) is: "I will be your God and you will be My people." This idea occurs a great number of times in Scripture.[7] The divine covenants establish a favorable relationship between God and His people. By means of the covenant, the covenant people become intimately related to the God of Creation and Redemption.

A Covenant Protects and Promotes Itself. Favorable covenantal relations are conditional. They are maintained only by a faithful keeping of the specified legal terms. Thus, of the covenant set

---

5. Exo. 31:18; 32:15; 34:1,4; Deut. 4:13. See Meredith G. Kline, "The Two Tables of the Covenant," chapter 1 in Part Two of *The Structure of Biblical Authority*, rev. ed. (Grand Rapids: Wm. B. Eerdmans, 1972), pp. 113-130.

6. Interestingly, in divine covenants the prophets were God's "lawyers." Their ministry involved prosecuting God's "lawsuit" against Israel for "breach of contract." For example, notice the legal terminology in Micah 6:1,2: "Hear now what the Lord is saying, Arise, *plead your case* before the mountains, and let the hills hear your voice. Listen, you mountains, to the *indictment* of the Lord, and you enduring foundations of the earth, because the Lord has a *case* against His people; even with Israel He will *dispute*." This explains, too, why "witnesses" were called to God's covenant. In Deuteronomy 30:19 Moses said, "I call heaven and earth to witness against you today" (Cp. Deut 4:26; 31:28; 32:1; Mic. 6:1,2).

7. Gen. 17:7; Exo. 5:2; 6:7; 29:45; Lev. 11:45; 26:12,45; Deut. 4:20; Deut. 7:9; 29:14-15; 2 Sam. 7:24; Psa. 105:9; Isa. 43:6; Jer. 24:7; 31:33; 32:38; Eze. 11:20; 34:24; 36:28; 37:23; Hos. 1:10; Zech. 8:8; 13:9; 2 Cor. 6:18; Rev. 21:3, 7.

before Israel in Deuteronomy 34:15,19, we read: "See, I have set before you today life and prosperity, and death and adversity. . . . I have set before you life and death, the blessing and the curse." Obedience to covenantal demands brings blessings; disobedience brings cursings.

A Covenant Is Solemnly and Formally Established. Covenants are not casual, informal, and inconsequential arrangements. They are established in a most solemn manner by means of designated symbolic actions. The manner in which they are established is quite significant. For instance, in Genesis 15 God sovereignly and graciously established His covenant with Abram by passing alone between the pieces of the animals Abram had sacrificed (Gen. 15:8-17). The symbolic covenantal action represented to Abram was a graphic "pledge-to-death" by God. He solemnly promised that He would perform His covenant promise, or else be "destroyed" (as were the sacrificial animals). Thus, in the Hebrew language the phrase "to make a covenant" may be translated literally: "to *cut* a covenant."

Formal Structure

Ancient sovereignly established covenants between imperial kings ("suzerains") and lesser kings and conquered nations and peoples ("vassals") often had a five-fold structure, generally found in the order below. A brief introduction to this structure will help us understand God's covenant, which also follows this covenantal pattern.[8]

1. *Transcendence*: Usually a preamble offering an introductory statement identifying the sovereignty of the covenant-making king.

2. *Hierarchy*: An historical prologue summarizing the king's authority and the mediation of his rule, by reminding of the historical circumstances of it.

3. *Ethics*: A detail of the legal stipulations defining the ethics of

---

8. More detailed information may be found in Ray Sutton, *That You May Prosper: Dominion By Covenant* (Tyler, TX: Institute for Christian Economics, 1987).

faithful living under the covenant bond.

4. *Oath*: The setting forth of the sanctions of the covenant, specifying the promises and the warnings of the covenant by the taking of a formal oath.

5. *Succession*: An explanation of the arrangements transferring the covenant to future generations.[9]

As I mentioned above, God's covenant follows the same pattern. As a matter of fact, this covenant structure appears frequently in the Bible. One prominent example is the entire book of Deuteronomy, which I will outline by way of illustration.[10]

1. *Transcendence* (specifying the sovereignty of the covenant making God). Deuteronomy 1:1-3 serves as the Preamble to the covenant detailed in Deuteronomy. In verse 3 Israel is told that Moses is delivering "all that the LORD had commanded him to give them." The English "LORD" translates the Hebrew "Jehovah," which occurs over 6000 times in the Old Testament. It was God's special, redemptive, covenantal name. By this name He made Himself known to Israel just prior to their glorious deliverance from Egypt (Exo. 6:2-7). The name Jehovah immediately spoke of God's exalted majesty and glorious might. This was He Who spoke and made covenant in Deuteronomy.

2. *Hierarchy* (specifying the mediation of the covenant maker's sovereign authority). In Deuteronomy 1:6-4:49 we discover a brief rehearsal of the covenantal history of Israel, which was to remind Israel of God's active, historical rule in world affairs. Let us notice three aspects of the hierarchy involved:

(1) The LORD was Israel's ultimate ruler. He graciously led and protected Israel in the wilderness and promised to overthrow their enemies in the Promised Land (Deut. 1:19-25, 29-31).

(2) Below the ultimate rulership of God was established the

---

9. The Greek word for "God" is *theos*. "THEOS" can serve as a handy acronym for remembering the identifying features of the covenant: Transcendence, Hierarchy, Ethics, Oath, and Succession.

10. For a more thorough investigation of this outline of Deuteronomy, see: Sutton, *That You May Prosper*, chs. 1-6.

immediate governance of Israel by elected elders (Deut. 1:12-16). These were to rule for God (Deut. 1:17).

(3) Under the direction of the government of Israel, the nation was to be an influential example to the nations of the goodness of God and His ultimate rule (Deut. 4:4-8). In essence, they were to be a light to the world,[11] ministering by hierarchical authority the rule of God in the world. Israel, as a body, was God's representative in the earth.

3. *Ethics* (specifying the stipulations of the covenant). In Deuteronomy the stipulations are found in chapters 5:1 through 26:19. At the head of this section stand the Ten Commandments (Deut. 5:1-21), which are the basic, fundamental law-principles of God. The other laws contained in Exodus, Deuteronomy, and elsewhere are "case laws," which illustrate how the "base law" is to apply under certain illustrative circumstances.[12]

4. *Oath* (specifying the solemn *sanctions* of the covenant). In Deuteronomy 27:1-30:20 the sanctions of the covenant are recorded. These sanctions encourage ethical conduct by promising reward and discourage ethical rebellion by threatening curse.

5. *Succession* (specifying the transfer of the covenantal arrangements into the future). In Deuteronomy 31-33 Moses is approaching death (31:2). He encourages future strength (31:6-8) and involvement of all the people, including the children (31:9-13). Obedience insures future continuity of blessing (32:46-47) upon all their tribes (33:1-29).

Clearly, the covenant idea is a fundamental concept in Scripture. Just as clearly the covenant is framed in concrete terms to

---

11. Isa. 42:6; 51:4; 60:3.

12. Interestingly, the structure of the stipulations section of Deuteronomy even follows the outline of the Ten Commandments: The first commandment is expanded upon in Deut. 6-11; the second commandment in Deut. 12-13; the third in Deut. 14; the fourth in Deut. 15:1-16:17; the fifth in Deut. 16:18-18:22; the sixth in 19:1-22:8; the seventh in Deut. 22:9-23:14; the eighth in Deut. 23:15-25:4; the ninth in Deut. 24:8-25:4; and the tenth in Deut. 25:5-26:19. See: James B. Jordan, *The Law of the Covenant: An Exposition of Exodus 21-23* (Tyler, TX: Institute for Christian Economics, 1984), pp. 199-206 and Sutton, *That You May Prosper*, App. 1. For additional, similar information, see: Walter Kaiser, *Toward Old Testament Ethics* (Grand Rapids: Zondervan, 1983), ch. 8.

avoid any confusion as to obligations and responsibilities.

The Covenant and the Great Commission

We come now to the heart of the matter: whether Christ's Great Commission is a covenant. If it is, then it will display the five-point structure of the biblical covenant model. There would be other indications of the covenantal aspects of His ministry. If the Great Commission really is a covenant, then all Christians come under its stipulations. They are required by God to work in history to carry it out.

The Christ of the Covenant

Christ is the fulfillment of the most basic promise of the covenant. In Him all the promises of God find their ultimate expression (1 Cor. 1:20).[13] He is the confirmation of the promises of God (Rom. 15:8). Thus, at His birth, the joy of God's covenant promise came to expression in inspired song in Zacharias' prophecy: "To perform the mercy promised to our fathers, and to remember his holy *covenant*" (Luke 1:72, emphasis added). The fundamental promise of the covenant ("I will be your God; you will be My people") comes to expression in the birth of the One called "Immanuel" ("God with us," Matt. 1:23), who came to "save His people from their sins" (Matt. 1:21).

Christ was self-consciously the "Messenger of the Covenant." This Messenger of the Covenant was prophesied in Malachi 3:1: "'Behold, I am going to send My messenger, and he will clear the way before Me. And the Lord, whom you seek, will suddenly come to His temple; and the messenger of the covenant, in whom you delight, behold, He is coming, says the Lord of hosts.'" That Christ comes as the Messenger of the Covenant is put beyond serious question in Christ's application of the first part of Malachi 3:1 to John the Baptist, who was Christ's forerunner. Matthew 11:10 records Christ's tribute to John: "This

---

13. See also: Acts 13:23, 32; 26:6.

is the one about whom it was written, 'Behold, I send My messenger before your face, who will prepare Your way before You.'" Thus, he cleared the way for the Messenger of the Covenant.

One of the longest recorded messages of Christ is the Sermon on the Mount (Matt. 5-7). Interestingly, Christ seems intentionally to parallel Himself with Moses, through whom came the Mosaic Covenant.[14] He does so by presenting Himself on the mountain (Matt. 5:1) as the Law Keeper (Matt. 5:15ff), in parallel with Moses on Mount Sinai as the Law Giver (Exo. 19-24).[15] Elsewhere, comparisons between Christ and Moses (or "Sinai") appear.[16]

Moses and Elijah, who represent the Law and the Prophets (the Old Covenant[17]), even appear somewhat later in Christ's ministry on the Mount of Transfiguration to cede their covenantal authority to Christ.[18] They spoke to Him regarding His soon coming departure from the world through death,[19] when He would formally establish the New Covenant.

The New Covenant was established by Christ, "the Messenger of the Covenant," in the Upper Room on the night preceding His crucifixion. It was established between Him and His New Covenant era people.[20] The New Covenant is the fruition (or "consummation"[21]) of the several progressive divine covenants, which developed God's redemptive plan in the Old Testament era.

---

14. Exo. 24:8; 34:27; Num. 14:44.

15. See: R. E. Nixon, *Matthew* in D. B. Guthrie and J. A. Motyer, eds., *The Eerdmans Bible Commentary* (3rd ed.: Grand Rapids: Wm. B. Eerdmans, 1970), p. 850. R. H. Fuller, "Matthew," in James L. Mays, ed., *Harper's Bible Commentary* (San Francisco: Harper and Row, 1988), p. 981. Robert H. Gundry, *Matthew: A Commentary on His Literary and Theological Art* (Grand Rapids: Wm. B. Eerdmans, 1982), pp. 593-596. Cp. William Hendriksen, *The Gospel of Matthew* (*New Testament Commentary*) (Grand Rapids: Baker, 1973), pp. 261ff.

16. John 1:17; Gal. 4:24-5:2; Heb. 3:2-5; 12:18-24.

17. 2 Cor. 3; Heb. 8; cp. Matt. 5:17.

18. Matt. 17:1-8; Mark 9:2-8; Luke 9:28-36. See also: 2 Pet. 1:17ff.

19. Luke 9:28-31.

20. The New Covenant is mentioned as established in Matt. 26:28; Mark 14:24; Luke 22:20; 1 Cor. 11:25; 2 Cor. 3:6ff; Heb. 8:8ff; 9:15ff; 12:24.

21. Robertson calls it "the Covenant of Consummation." Robertson, *The Christ of the Covenants*, ch. 13.

It is clear that Christ presents Himself as the Messenger of the Covenant to establish the final consummative covenant between God and His people. And this is significant for understanding the Great Commission as a covenantal transaction.

The Commission and the Covenant

I have spent these several pages developing the covenant theme of Scripture in order to put the Great Commission in covenantal perspective. The Great Commission is a summary of the New Covenant. Consequently, we discover in it the specific structuring features so characteristic of covenants. At this juncture we will just briefly suggest the covenantal elements of the Great Commission. These will be exhibited in detail in Part II of this study.

The basic structure of the Great Commission involves the following elements:

1. *Transcendent sovereignty.* Christ gives the Commission from a mountain setting, an environment so characteristic of exaltedness in Scripture. "The eleven disciples proceeded to Galilee, to the mountain which Jesus had designated" (Matt. 28:16).

2. *Hierarchical authority.* From the mountain top Christ declares all authority in heaven and earth is His. He then commissions His followers to make His authority known and felt throughout the earth. "And when they saw Him, they worshiped Him. . . . And Jesus came up and spoke to them, saying, 'All authority has been given to Me in heaven and on earth. Go therefore and make disciples of all the nations'" (Matt. 28:17a, 18-19a).

3. *Ethical stipulations.* Those who are bound to Him in baptism are to learn and obey the stipulations of their sovereign, Christ Jesus. "Make disciples of all the nations. . . . Teach them to observe all that I commanded you" (Matt. 28:19a, 20a).

4. *Oath commitment.* Those to be brought under the gracious sway of Christ's authority should be baptized in His Name, as a pledge of covenantal allegiance to Him. "[Baptize] them in the name of the Father and the Son and the Holy Spirit" (Matt. 28:19b).

5. *Succession arrangements.* Christ establishes His commission for the extension of His authority through space ("all nations," Matt. 28:19b) and through time ("And, lo, I am with you always, even to the end of the age," Matt. 28:20b).

Conclusion

The repeated emphasis of Scripture on covenant cannot be denied. Our God is a covenant-making God, who speaks and acts in history among men. The redemption He provides in Christ cannot properly and fully be understood apart from the covenantal progress exhibited in Scripture. Neither may our tasks as Christians be properly grasped apart from the covenant. As we shall see, the covenant framework of the Great Commission holds within it the essence of the Christian enterprise, of the Christian's calling in the world.

May we dedicate ourselves to that task, as we come to a better comprehension of it.

Part II

CONFIGURATION

I. Covenantal Transcendence

3

THE DECLARATION OF SOVEREIGNTY

The eleven disciples proceeded to Galilee, to the mountain which Jesus had designated. And when they saw Him, they worshiped Him (Matthew 28:16-17a).

The first point of the covenant model is the establishment of the *sovereignty* of the covenant maker. As we approach the Great Commission from a covenantal perspective, we discover that its contextual setting clearly points to its sovereign disposition in a number of ways.

As we begin our study of the matter, we must recognize that the books of Scripture were written by real, flesh-and-blood, historical men under the inspiration of the Holy Spirit. Thus the books were given in particular, concrete historical contexts (2 Pet. 1:21).[1] The Scriptures did not fall from heaven as a book of mysteries. Consequently, at least a general understanding of the historical and geographical contexts of any given passage is helpful to its fuller and more accurate apprehension.

In addition to being aware of the historical and geographical contexts of any given passage, it is often helpful to understand something of the literary structure of the particular book of Scripture in which it is found. This is especially true of the Gospels, which represent a new literary genre that is neither biography nor theology. This literary genre is "gospel." As New

---

1. See the emphasis on the historical, for example, in Isa. 7:3; Zech. 1:1; Luke 2:1,2; 3:1-3.

Testament theologian Donald B. Guthrie has noted of the Gospels: "Whereas they are historical in form, their purpose was something more than historical. It is not, in fact, an accident that they were called 'Gospels' at an early period in Christian history . . . . [T]here were no parallels to the Gospel form which served as a pattern for the earliest writers."[2] The Gospels were written by common men, who organized the material according to a thought-out structure, plan, and purpose (cf. Luke 1:1-4).[3] So something of the literary structure of Matthew will also be helpful in opening to us the sovereignty of the covenantal Great Commission. Let us consider, then, the place, time, and literary setting of the Commission.

The Geographical Context

As we turn to the geographical matter, we will note the covenantal significance of both the region and the topography of the place where the Commission was given. The region was in "Galilee"; the topographical setting was on a "mountain."

Galilee

The Gospels teach us that Christ's disciples were instructed by Him to go a certain, specified place in *Galilee* to meet Him after the resurrection.[4] And, of course, the Matthew 28:16 reference is from the very context of the Great Commission.

It is interesting that Christ instructs His disciples to meet him in *Galilee*.[5] Of course, Christ lived there in His youth,[6]

---

2. Donald B. Guthrie, *New Testament Introduction* (3rd ed.: Downers Grove, IL: Inter-Varsity Press, 1970), pp. 13-14. See also F. F. Bruce, *Bulletin of the John Rylands Library*, xlv (1963), pp. 319-339; C. F. D. Moule, *The Birth of the New Testament* (3rd. ed.: San Francisco: Harper and Row, 1982), ch. 5; and A. E. J. Rawlinson, *The Gospel according to St. Mark*, Westminster Commentary (7th ed.: London: Macmillan, 1949), pp. xviiiff.
3. Notice, for instance, the structure of John's Gospel around seven miracles and Matthew's around five major discourses, which alternate narrative and discourse. See: Robert H. Gundry, *New Testament Introduction* (Grand Rapids: Zondervan, 1970), pp. 29ff, 309ff.
4. Mark 16:7; Matt. 26:32; 28:7, 10, 16.
5. There has been an intense scholarly debate on this appearance in Galilee in an effort to harmonize it with Luke's record of Christ's appearing in Jerusalem in Judea. The time and effort required to move back and forth between the two regions is part of

called His disciples in Galilee,[7] and performed much of His ministry there. Yet the fact that He would prearrange a post-resurrection appearance with His disciples in Galilee in order to commission them as He does, is instructive. This change of locale is noteworthy in that they were already in *Jerusalem*, the heart of Israel in Judea, and were very soon to return there to await the Pentecostal empowerment for their mission.[8] Why were they now instructed to take the trip to *Galilee*?

Galilee was an area in Israel that contained *a mixed Jew and gentile population* from the earliest times, having been only inadequately conquered and settled by the Jews during the original conquest of the Promised Land (Jdgs. 1:33). In addition, during the later Assyrian conflict, the Jews of the area were carried off into captivity, leaving many gentiles as the inhabitants of the land (2 Kgs. 15:29). For these reasons, Upper Galilee was known as "Galilee *of the gentiles*."[9] Also for these reasons, Galileans were noted for their peculiar mixed accent,[10] and were looked down upon by the Jews in the southern, more "pure" regions.[11]

Interestingly, Matthew is the only Gospel that mentions Christ's early command for the disciples to avoid the gentiles in their ministry,[12] refers to Jerusalem as "the holy city,"[13] and records Christ's being called the "king of the Jews" prior to Pilate's cross inscription.[14] Yet three times at the end of this Gospel Matthew mentions that Christ was to meet His disciples in *Galilee*, well away from Jerusalem and well into the area of mixed Jew and gentile inhabitants.[15]

In addition to this information, we should note that just

---

the problem in attempting to construct a chronology of the events.
6. Matt. 2:22-23.
7. Matt. 4:18-22; John 1:43-44.
8. Luke 24:47, 49, 52; Acts 1:4, 8, 12.
9. Isa. 9:1; Matt. 4:13,15,16.
10. Matt. 26:73; Mark 14:70; Acts 2:7.
11. Luke 13:1; John 1:46; 4:45; 7:52; Acts 2:7.
12. Matt. 10:5,6; 15:2-4.
13. Matt. 4:5; 27:53.
14. Matt. 2:2.
15. Matt. 28:7, 10, 16.

prior to the Great Commission is mentioned the Jewish bribe and the lie regarding the whereabouts of Christ's body: "They gave a large sum of money to the soldiers, and said, 'You are to say, "his disciples came by night and stole Him away while we were asleep.' . . . And they took the money and did as they had been instructed; and this story was widely spread among the *Jews*, and is to this day."[16] Upon mention of this cover-up by the *Jews* in Jerusalem, Christ appears in *Galilee* to give His commission to "disciple the *nations*" (Matt. 28:16, 19). The gospel, as we will see, was designed to promote Christ's sovereignty over the entire world of men, not just the Jews. Thus, even the *place* of its giving anticipates this, for "in light of [Matt. 4:15ff] it is likely that Galilee here represents *all peoples* in vs. 19."[17]

The Mountain

That the disciples went "to the *mountain* which Jesus had designated"[18] seems also to be for some particular purpose. Christ's employment of mountains for instructional effect is familiar enough. For instance, the Sermon on the Mount, the Olivet Discourse, and the ascension were from a mountain — the Mount of Olives.[19]

Mountains are significant in Scripture as *symbols of sovereignty, majesty, exaltation, and power*.[20] As such, they often stand for kingdoms, as several of the verses in the preceding note sug-

---

16. Matt. 28:12, 13, 15.

17. W. F. Albright and C. S. Mann, *Matthew: The Anchor Bible* (Garden City, New York: Doubleday, 1971), p. 361. See also: J. Knox Chamblin, *Matthew* in W. A. Elwell, ed., *Evangelical Bible Commentary on the Bible* (Grand Rapids: Baker, 1989), pp. 779-780.

18. Emphasis mine. The fact that "the mountain" is not mentioned in any other context where Galilee is specified as the destination of these disciples has been a source of discussion among commentators (Mark 16:7; Matt. 28:7, 10, 16). Nevertheless, the text *here* clearly does so. Several commentators suggest it is the same one in which the Sermon on the Mount was given: Chamblin, *Matthew*, p. 780. R. E. Nixon, *Matthew*, in D. B. Guthrie and J. A. Motyer, eds., *The Eerdmans Bible Commentary* (3rd ed: Grand Rapids: 1970), p. 850. F. C. Cook, *New Testament*, 1:194. Robert H. Gundry, *Matthew: A Commentary on His Literary an Theological Art* (Grand Rapids: Wm. B. Eerdmans, 1982), p. 594.

19. Matt. 5-7; 24:3; Acts 1:11,12.

20. For example, Isa. 2:2-3; 11:9; 25:6; Eze. 17:22; 20:40; Dan. 2:35; Mic. 4:1; Zech. 4:7. See: David Chilton, *Paradise Restored: A Biblical Theology of Dominion* (Ft. Worth, Texas: Dominion Press, 1985), ch. 4.

gest. It was on a mountain that Christ commissioned His disciples to take the gospel to "the nations." The majestic effect of this commissioning from a mountain will be dealt with in detail later in Chapter 4. There I will focus on the implications of the hierarchical authority of the commission. At this point, I merely point out the appropriateness of the majestic commissioning of the disciples from a mountain for symbolizing His sovereign transcendence in this covenantal transaction.

The idea is captured well by Lenski: "On mountain heights heaven and earth, as it were, meet, and here the glorified Savior spoke of his power in heaven and on earth. With the vast expanse of the sky above him and the great panorama of the earth spread beneath him, Jesus stands in his exaltation and his glory — a striking vision, indeed."[21] This is why the disciples "worshiped" Him there (Matt. 28:17a).

The Temporal Context

The Commission was granted by the *resurrected* Savior Who had "finished" (John 19:30)[22] the work of redemption, which His Father gave Him to do (John 17:4). Having conquered sin (Rom. 3:23-26), Satan (Col. 2:15), and death (Acts 2:24, 31), Christ arose victoriously from the tomb as a conquering king[23] to commission His disciples with sovereign authority to take this message to "all nations." In the complex of events connecting the resurrection and the Great Commission, we witness the investiture of Christ as sovereign.

It was particularly *at the resurrection* that Christ was "declared to be the Son of God with power," according to Paul in Romans 1:4. That verse reads: He was "declared to be the Son of God with power, according to the spirit of holiness, by the resurrection from the dead." Actually the word translated "declared"[24]

---

21. R. C. H. Lenski, *The Interpretation of St. Matthew's Gospel* (Columbus, OH: Wartburg Press, 1943), p. 1168.
22. Cp. John 4:34; Heb. 1:3; 9:26-27.
23. See discussion of His kingship, below, pp. 39-40, 102-3.
24. In the Greek: *horisthentos* (from *horizo*). It is found elsewhere in Luke 22:22; Acts 2:23; 10:42; 11:29; 17:26, 31; Heb. 4:7. For an excellent exposition of Romans 1:4 see: John Murray, *The Epistle to the Romans* (New International Commentary on the New Testament),

in most translations of Romans 1:4 is never translated thus elsewhere. The word is generally understood to mean: "determine, appoint, ordain." As Murray notes: "There is neither need nor warrant to resort to any other rendering than that provided by the other New Testament instances, namely, that Christ was 'appointed' or 'constituted' Son of God with power and points therefore to an investiture which had an historical beginning parallel to the historical beginning mentioned in" Romans 1:3.[25]

Of course, Christ was not "appointed" the Son of God. But on this recommended reading, Romans 1:4 does not suggest that; it says He was "appointed the Son of God *with power.*" The very point of Romans 1 is that Christ came *in history* as the "seed of David" (Rom. 1:3), not that He dwelled in eternity as the Son of God. Thus, at the resurrection, Christ "was *instated* in a position of sovereignty and invested with power, an event which in respect of investiture with power surpassed everything that could previously be ascribed to him in his incarnate state."[26]

Returning to Matthew 28:18, we should note that a literal rendering of the verse reads: "And having come near, Jesus spake to them, saying, 'Given to me was all authority . . . .'"[27] Both the position and the tense of the word "given" should be noted. In Greek, words thrown to the front of a sentence are generally emphasized — as "given" is here in Christ's statement. Not only is "given" emphasized as being particularly significant, but according to the Greek verb tense,[28] His being "given" authority was at some point in *past time.*

---

2 vols. (Grand Rapids: Wm. B. Eerdmans, 1959, 1965), 1:9. The Revised Standard Version and The Amplified Bible translate the verb: "designated."

25. *Ibid.*

26. *Ibid.*, 1:10.

27. Robert Young, *Young's Literal Translation of the Holy Bible* (Grand Rapids: Baker, rep. n.d. [1898]), New Testament, p. 23.

28. The Greek for "given" is *edothe*, which is the aorist passive indicative of *didomi.* The word "aorist" is made up of two Greek words: *a* ("no") and *horizo* ("horizon"), which means "unlimited." Normally, therefore, an aorist tense has no temporal connotation. In the indicative tense, however, it carries the connotation of a past action conceived as in a point of time.

The point at which this grant of authority occurred was obviously at the resurrection, according not only to the clear implication of the text before us, but also to the confirmation in Romans 1:4: "Who was declared the Son of God with power by the resurrection from the dead, according to the Spirit of holiness, Jesus Christ our Lord."[29] The resurrection, followed shortly by the ascension, established Christ as King and enthroned Him as such. We should note that Philippians 2:8,9 also uses the same tense[30] to point to the resurrection as that time when Christ was "bestowed" authority: "He humbled Himself by becoming obedient to the point of death, even death on a cross. Therefore also God highly exalted Him, and *bestowed* on Him the name which is above every name."

For this reason, J. P. Lange has designated the Great Commission a "second transfiguration."[31] As Calvin wrote of the Lord's statement in Matthew 28:18: "We must note, His Authority was not openly displayed until He rose from the dead. Only then did He advance aloft, wearing the insignia of supreme King."[32] From this time forth, we cease to hear His familiar "I can do nothing of Myself,"[33] for now "all authority" is rightfully His.

Furthermore, this grant of kingly authority was prophesied in Psalm 2:6-7:

---

29. Of course, it is true in terms of His *essential deity* that this "all authority given" was "not as a new gift, but a *confirmation* and *practical* realisation of the power over all things, which had been delivered unto Him by the Father" as regards His human existence. F. C. Cook, ed., *New Testament*, vol. 1: *St. Matthew—St. Mark—St. Luke*, in *The Holy Bible According to the Authorized Version A.D. (1611), With an Explanatory and Critical Commentary and a Revision of the Translation* (New York: Charles Scribner's Sons, 1901), p. 196. Emphasis added.

30. Philippians 2:9, however, employs a different word for "given": *echarisato* from *charizomai*.

31. John Peter Lange, *Matthew* in Philip Schaff, ed. and transl., *Commentary on the Holy Scripture, Critical, Doctrinal and Homiletical* (3rd ed.: Grand Rapids: Zondervan, n.d. [1861]), p. 556.

32. John Calvin, *A Harmony of the Gospels Matthew, Mark, and Luke*, in *Calvin's New Testament Commentaries*, ed. by David W. and Thomas F. Torrance, trans. by A. W. Morrison, 3 Vols., (Grand Rapids: Wm. B. Eerdmans, 1972), 3:250.

33. John 5:19, 30; 8:28; 12:49; 14:10.

I will surely tell of the decree of the Lord;
He said to Me, 'Thou art My Son,
Today I have begotten Thee.
Ask of Me, and I will surely give the nations as Thine inheritance,
And the very ends of the earth as Thy possession.'

In Acts this passage from Psalm 2 is clearly applied to the resurrection of Christ. Acts 13:33-34 reads: "God has fulfilled this
promise to our children in that He raised up Jesus, as it is also
written in the second Psalm, 'Thou art My Son; Today I have
begotten Thee.' And as for the fact that He raised Him up from
the dead, no more to return to decay . . . ."

Though not referring to Psalm 2, Acts 2:30-31 agrees that
the resurrection of Christ was to kingly authority: "And so,
because [David] was a prophet, and knew that God had sworn
to him with an oath to seat one of his descendants upon his
throne, he looked ahead and spoke of the resurrection of the
Christ . . . ." Then Peter, making reference to Psalm 110, adds:
"For it was not David who ascended into heaven, but he himself
says: 'The Lord said to My Lord, Sit at My right hand, Until I
make Thine enemies a footstool for Thy feet'" (Acts 2:34b-35).

Turning back to Matthew 28:18, we should note that Christ's
statement indicates something new has occurred as the result of
the completion of His redemptive work at His resurrection
from the grave. He has *now* been given "all authority." The
wondrous significance of this will be demonstrated below.

Christ is our prophet, priest, and king,[34] and His Great
Commission exhibits His manifold ministry to His people.[35]
Thus, in this and the following chapter, we will see that He
speaks as the *Great King*, who rules over His vast kingdom, in
that He has "all authority in heaven and on earth" (Matt.
28:18b).[36] He is "the King of kings and Lord of lords" (Rev.

---

34. The one verse that most clearly brings together these three offices is Rev. 1:5:
"And from Jesus Christ the faithful witness [prophet], the firstborn of the dead [priest],
and the ruler of the kings of the earth [king]."

35. "As Prophet He represents God with man; as Priest He represents man in the
presence of God; and as King He exercises dominion and restores the original dominion
of man." Louis Berkhof, *Systematic Theology* (4th ed.: Grand Rapids: Wm. B. Eerdmans,
1941), p. 357.

36. For an excellent treatment of Christ's present kingship, see William Symington,

19:16). In Chapter Five we will see how the Great Commission is also a prophetic Commission. As the *Great Prophet*, Christ declares the will of God for all the world, by teaching men "to observe all that I commanded" (Matt. 28:20a). In Chapter Six, the priestly aspect of the Commission will become evident. As the *Great High Priest*, He secures the worshipful oaths of those over whom it holds sway, in His command to "baptize" the nations (Matt. 28:19b).

The Literary Context

The beautiful structure of Matthew's Gospel merits our attention as we consider the Great Commission. Blair comments regarding Matthew 28:18ff: "Here many of the emphases of the book are caught up."[37] Cook concurs: "With this sublime utterance St. Matthew winds up his Gospel, throughout which he has kept the principles, which are thus enunciated, distinctly before our minds."[38]

I would go a step further and note that what we read in the *closing* words of Matthew's Gospel in the closing days of Christ's ministry has already been anticipated in the *opening* words of the Gospel and of Christ's earthly life and the beginning of His ministry. Thus, the very opening chapters of Matthew seem to expect the conclusion we get in the Great Commission. Let me just briefly draw out the parallels; they do not seem to be merely coincidental. They speak of *a King who comes* (Matt. 1-4) and *receives sovereignty* (Matt. 28) over a kingdom.

1. *Jesus as "Immanuel."* A. In the birth announcement to Joseph, we have the angelic declaration of the fulfillment of Isaiah 7:14 in Jesus's birth: "Behold, the virgin shall be with child, and shall bear a Son, and they shall call His name Immanuel,"

Messiah the Prince or, The Mediatorial Dominion of Jesus Christ (Edmonton, Alberta: Still Waters Revival, rep. 1990 [1884]). See also: Greg L. Bahnsen and Kenneth L. Gentry, Jr., *House Divided: The Break-up of Dispensational Theology* (Tyler, TX: Institute for Christian Economics, 1989), ch. 12. John Jefferson Davis, *Christ's Victorious Kingdom: Postmillennialism Reconsidered* (Grand Rapids: Baker, 1984), ch. 4.

37. Edward P. Blair, *Jesus in the Gospel of Matthew* (New York: Abingdon, 1960), p. 45.

38. F. C. Cook, *St. Matthew*, p. 45.

which translated means, *'God with us'* " (Matt. 1:23). "God with us" has come! B. In the conclusion of Matthew and in the Great Commission, we have the same theme: "And, lo, *I am with you always*" (Matt. 28:20b). "God with us" remains!

2. *The Royalty of Jesus.* A. In Matthew 1:1 the royal genealogy of Christ is pushed forward: "The book of the genealogy of Jesus Christ, the son of David, the son of Abraham."[39] Here not only do we have Christ's human name ("Jesus") coupled with His Messianic name ("Christ"), but with the royal title "Son of David," a familiar Messianic ascription in Matthew.[40] Thus: "The genealogy presented in Matt. 1:1-17 is not an appendix but is closely connected with the substance of the entire chapter; in a broader sense, with the contents of the entire book."[41]

B. In Matthew 28:18 Christ comes to His disciples in the exercise of His recently secured royal authority: "All authority is given Me in heaven and on earth." A fitting conclusion to a work opening with a royal genealogy.

3. *Gentiles and the King.* A. In Matthew 2:1ff we read of *gentile* magi coming from "the east" in search of Christ. They seek Him "who has been born King of the Jews" (Matt. 2:2a). B. In Matthew 28:19 we read of the sovereign King with "all authority in heaven and earth" sending His disciples in search of the gentiles: "Go, make disciples of all the nations."[42]

---

39. As has been said, "This first sentence is equivalent to a formal declaration of our Lord's Messiahship." J. A. Alexander, *The Gospel According to Matthew* (Grand Rapids: Baker, [1860] 1980), p. 2.

40. See: Matthew 9:27; 12:23; 15:22; 20:30; 21:9, 15; 22:42. The very structure of this genealogy hinges on "David the king" (Matt. 1:6a). Its self-conscious division into fourteen generations (Matt. 1:17) uses David twice as a pivot: The genealogy is traced with an upbeat thrust from Abraham to David, who closes the first cycle (Matt. 1:6). Then from David (Matt. 1:6b) downward (in decline) to the Babylonian Captivity (Matt. 1:11). Then it moves again upward to Christ (Matt. 1:16-17).

41. William Hendriksen, *The Gospel According to Matthew* (Grand Rapids: Baker, 1973), p. 107.

42. Interestingly, the opening verse of Matthew is: "The book of the genealogy of Jesus Christ, the son of David, *the son of Abraham.*" In Genesis 12:3 similar terminology to Matt. 28:19 is found in referring to "all the nations." Reflecting back on the Genesis 12:3, Paul writes: "And the Scripture, foreseeing that God would justify the Gentiles by faith, preached the gospel beforehand to Abraham, saying, *'All the nations* shall be blessed in you' " (Gal. 3:8; the language here is identical to Matt. 28:19). Consequently, in the closing verses of Matthew we see the means of that blessing for "all the nations": the

4. *Christ Attacked.* A. In Matthew 2 we read of a king's attempted destruction of the young Jesus toward the beginning of His earthly sojourn: "Herod is going to search for the Child to destroy Him" (Matt. 2:13b). B. The Great Commission was given after the final attempted destruction of Christ by means of the crucifixion (Matt. 27:33ff) toward the end of His earthly ministry.

5. *Israel Replaced by the Nations.* A. In Matthew 3:9-11 John Baptist warns the Jews in Judea, who were so proud of their Abrahamic descent,[43] that "the axe is already laid at the root of the trees" and that there was coming a fiery destruction of Jerusalem. B. In the Great Commission, Christ, the true Son of Abraham, while in Galilee (v. 16) after the Jews lied about His resurrection (vv. 12-15), commands His followers to "Go therefore and make disciples of all the nations" (Matt. 28:19).

6. *Geographical Juxtaposition.* A. In Matthew 3 Christ's first public appearance opens with these words: "Then Jesus arrived from Galilee at the Jordan" (Matt. 3:13). His movement was from Galilee to Judea (Matt. 3:1). B. In the closing of Matthew and His ministry as recorded there, Christ's movement is the opposite: He moves from Jerusalem in Judea to Galilee (Matt. 28:1, 6-7, 10, 16).

7. *Baptismal Ritual.* A. As Christ's public presentation opens in Matthew, we read: "Then Jesus arrived from Galilee at the Jordan coming to John, to be baptized by him" (Matt. 3:13). B. In the closing of Christ's ministry in Matthew, we read: "Go therefore and make disciples of all the nations, baptizing them" (Matt. 28:19).

8. *The Trinity.* A. At Christ's baptism we have one of the Scripture's clearest evidences of the Trinity: "After being baptized, Jesus [the Son] went up immediately from the water; and behold, the heavens were opened, and he saw the Spirit of God [the Holy Spirit] descending as a dove, and coming upon Him, and behold, a voice out of the heavens [the Father], saying, 'This is My beloved Son, in whom I am well-pleased'" (Matt.

Great Commission.
43. Matt. 3:9; John 8:33, 39.

3:16-17). B. In Christ's baptismal formula in the Great Commission, we again have clearly reflected the Trinity: "baptizing them in the name of the Father and the Son and the Holy Spirit" (Matt. 28:19).

9. *The Mountain.* A. Before Christ formally begins His ministry, He endures the temptation by Satan in Matthew 4. There we read of the role of a "mountain" in the temptation to kingship: "The devil took Him to a very high mountain, and showed Him all the kingdoms of the world, and their glory" (Matt. 4:8). B. In the Great Commission, Christ speaks from a mountain with newly won royal authority: "the eleven disciples proceeded to Galilee, to the mountain which Jesus had designated" (Matt. 28:16).

10. *Kingdom Given.* A. In the temptation at the opening of the ministry of the Prophet, Priest, and King,[44] Jesus Christ, Satan offers to give Him the kingdoms of the world: "The devil took Him to a very high mountain, and showed Him all the kingdoms of the world, and their glory; and he said to Him, 'All these things will I give You, if. . .'." (Matt. 4:8-9). B. In the concluding Great Commission, Christ sovereignly declares that He had been "given"[45] "all authority," not only over the kingdoms Satan had authority over, but also in heaven: "All authority has been given to Me in heaven and on earth" (Matt. 28:18).

11. *Worship.* A. In the temptation, Satan seeks Christ's worship of him: "All these things will I give You, if You will fall down and worship me" (Matt. 4:8). B. In the Great Commission, we read that Christ receives worship[46]: "And when they

---

44. Following forty days of fasting, the first temptation to turn stones to bread (Matt. 4:2-3) reminds us of the *prophet* Moses (cf. Deut. 18:18), who fasted forty days and nights (Exo. 24:28). The second temptation (in Matthew's order) was on the temple, wherein the *priests* ministered (Matt. 4:5). The third temptation on the mountain was for Him to become *king* over "the kingdoms of the world" (Matt. 4:8-9).

45. The same word "give" (from the Greek: *didomi*) is used in two temptation accounts (Matt. 4:9; Luke 4:6) and in the Great Commission (Matt. 28:18). Luke's Gospel records more detail of this temptation, where Satan says: "To thee I will *give all* this *authority*, and their glory, because to me it hath been delivered" (*Young's Literal Translation*, New Testament, p. 42). Compare this to Christ's "*All authority* has been *given* to Me."

46. The same Greek word for "worship" is employed in both places (Greek: *proskuneo*).

saw Him, they worshiped Him" (Matt. 28:17).

12. *His Disciples.* A. In Matthew 4:18 Christ calls His first disciples as His earthly ministry begins. B. In Matthew 28:18-20 He commissions His disciples as His earthly ministry ends.

The Gospel of Matthew is the larger literary context of the Great Commission. In this Gospel the sovereign kingship of Christ is initially anticipated (Matt. 1-4) and finally secured (Matt. 28:18-20). The literary (by inspiration) and the historical (by providence) paralleling of the beginning and end well support the notion that the Great Commission is a royal commission establishing the sovereignty of the "King of kings and Lord of lords."

Conclusion

During Christ's ministry, the long-prophesied kingdom came "near"[47] and was gradually established in the world,[48] as was intended.[49] Consequently, men were pressing into it at His preaching.[50] After He declares it judicially accomplished ("all authority" was given Him, Matt. 28:18) and after His formal coronation at His ascension into heaven,[51] we read of later Christians declaring Him king[52] and entering His kingdom.[53] Christ today rules from the right hand of the throne of God.[54]

The geographical, temporal, and literary contexts of the Great Commission all move us to recognize its royal dignity, its covenantal assertion of *sovereignty*. Upon the securing of His kingdom, the King of heaven and earth speaks of His kingdom task as He commissions His disciples. The kingdom that had been making advances in the ministry of Christ was judicially secured by right at the resurrection.

---

47. Mark 1:14-15; 9:1; Luke 21:31; Matt. 3:2; 4:12-17; 10:7; 16:28.
48. Matt. 12:28; Luke 17:20-21.
49. Isa. 9:6,7; Luke 1:31-33; Matt. 2:2; John 12:12-15; 18:36-37.
50. Matt. 11:12; Luke 16:16. Phillips translates Matt. 11:12: "From the days of John the Baptist until now the kingdom of Heaven has been taken by storm and eager men are forcing their way into it."
51. Acts 2:30-31, 33-36; Heb. 2:9.
52. Acts 3:15; 5:31; 17:7.
53. Col. 1:12-13; 1 Thess. 2:12; Rev. 1:6, 9.
54. Rom. 8:34; Eph. 1:20; Col. 3:1; Heb. 12:2; 1 Pet. 3:22; Rev. 3:21.

To understand the Great Commission as anything less than the recognition of the sovereign dignity of Christ and the outline of His kingdom expansion falls short of the greatness of the Great Commission. As the first point of a covenantal transaction is the establishment of the covenant maker's sovereignty, so in the Great Commission we see Christ exhibited as the sovereign Lord, declaring His sovereignty from a mountain top.

4

THE EXERCISE OF SOVEREIGNTY

And Jesus came up and spoke to them, saying, "All authority has been given to Me in heaven and on earth. Go therefore and make disciples of all the nations" (Matthew 28:18-19a).

As I noted in Chapter Three, the Great Commission is a *kingly* commission exhibiting the sovereignty of the King of kings and Lord of lords.

In this chapter we will look more closely at the *implications* of the sovereign, kingly authority-grant received by Christ, which is the legal basis of the Great Commission. As we do so, we will discover the mediation of the authority of that covenantal sovereignty.

Covenantal hierarchy is clearly set forth in Matthew 28:18-19a (cited above). Here we may trace the hierarchical flow of authority:

(1) Authority is original in and derivative from the Triune God ("all authority has been given," obviously by God).

(2) Mediatorial authority is granted as a redemptive reward to the God-Man, Jesus Christ ("to Me").

(3) Christ commissions Christians administratively to promote obedience to that authority ("Go therefore").[1]

---

1. This underscores the Christian's covenantal status in history. See Matt. 5:5; 1 Cor.

(4) Self-conscious submission to that authority is to spread to all the world ("make disciples of all the nations").

This is why the heralds of Christ's kingdom are called "ambassadors."[2] In the Great Commission the claim of Christ to have received from God "all authority in heaven and on earth" formalizes *judicially* what was already true metaphysically: God's rulership over all.[3] That is, Christ in His eternal Person as God the Son always possesses authority in Himself; it is intrinsic to His very divine being.[4] But in terms of the *economy of redemption* (the outworking of salvation), the Second Person of the Trinity humbled Himself from His exalted position and made Himself of "no reputation" (Phil. 2:7) by taking on a human body and soul.[5] He did this in order to secure redemption for His people, by living under the *Law* and suffering the *judicial consequences* of its breach by them.[6] The *judicial declaration* of the acceptance of His redemptive labor by the Father was at the resurrection, which historical event led to His being granted "all authority" as a conquering King.

But what is entailed in this grant of "all authority in heaven and on earth"? And what is to be the outreach program of the

---

3:21-23; Eph. 1:3; 2:6.

2. 2 Cor. 5:20; Eph. 6:20. Some scholars suggest a slight misspelling in the text of Philemon 9 that allows the word "aged" (*presbutes*) to be rendered "ambassador" (*presbeutes*), as well. For example, J. B. Lightfoot, C. F. D. Moule, B. F. Westcott, F. J. A. Hort, E. Haupt, E. Lohmeyer, W. O. E. Oesterley, and George Abbott-Smith. See: W. F. Arndt and F. W. Gingrich, *A Greek-English Lexicon of the New Testament and Other Early Christian Literature* (Chicago: University of Chicago, 1957), p. 707.

3. Despite the recent shift in evangelicalism from a judicial to a love-based approach, the judicial element in Scripture is extremely strong. For a brief discussion of this distressing paradigm shift, see: Robert Brow, "Evangelical Megashift," *Christianity Today* (February, 1990) 12-17. See also: Gary North, *Political Polytheism: The Myth of Pluralism* (Tyler, TX: Institute for Christian Economics, 1989), pp. 631-643.

4. In fact, the Greek word for "authority" is *exousia*, which is derived etymologically from *ek* ("out of") and *ousia* ("being").

5. Notice the hierarchical order in 1 Cor. 11:3: "But I would have you know, that the head of every man is Christ; and the head of the woman is the man; and the head of Christ is God."

6. See: Matt. 20:28; Mark 10:45; John 1:14; Rom. 1:3; 8:3; 15:8; 2 Cor. 8:9; Gal. 3:10ff; 4:4; Phil. 2:5-11; Heb. 2:9-17; 10:5; 12:2.

Church based on this grant?

The Source of Authority

The One who issues this Great Commission to His people is He who possesses "all authority in heaven and in earth." This same terminology is applied to God the Father Himself: He is "the Lord of heaven and earth" (Matt. 11:25). God is Lord and Governor of all.[7] Strong Pharaoh was raised up so that he might be destroyed, in order to bring glory to God (Exo. 9:16). The mighty Assyrian Empire was but a rod of anger in His hand.[8] The powerful Babylonian king, Nebuchadnezzar, was His "servant."[9] The conquering Persian king, Cyrus, was used by God as a "Shepherd" and as "His anointed" for God's holy purpose.[10] The Medes were His own weapon.[11] Indeed, He is the King of all the earth.[12]

God's Lordship is unbounded in Scripture. And Christ lays claim to that boundless authority in the Great Commission. Hence, the divine nature of the Commission. It is not an authority bestowed ecclesiastically, traditionally, philosophically, or politically, but a divinely derived one. The Great Commission comes to us with a very bold statement: "Thus saith the *Lord*."

The resurrection was the first step in Christ's exaltation; the ascension His concluding step.[13] In fact, "The ascension is essentially implied in the resurrection. Both events are combined in the one fact of Christ's exaltation. The resurrection is the root and the beginning of the ascension; the ascension is the blossom and crown of the resurrection. . . The resurrection marks the entrance into the heavenly *state*; the

---

7. Amos 1:3-2:3; Oba. 1; Isa. 10:5-34.
8. Isa. 10:5.
9. Jer. 25:9; 27:6; 43:10. See also: Jer. 51:20.
10. Isa. 44:28-45:13.
11. Jer. 51:11, 20.
12. Psa. 29:10; 47:2; 95:3; 96:10; 97:10; 103:19; 115:3; 145:11-13; Dan. 2:47; 4:35; Isa. 6:5; Jer. 46:18.
13. John Peter Lange, *Matthew* (3rd ed.), in *Commentary on the Holy Scriptures Critical, Doctrinal and Homiletical*, ed. and trans. by Philip Schaff (Grand Rapids: Zondervan, rep. n.d. [1861]), 15:561-562.

ascension, into the heavenly *sphere*."[14]

Within days of the resurrection, Christ completed His two-phased exaltation, when He ascended into heaven in fulfillment of Daniel 7:13, 14. This passage is quite important in this regard, though often misconstrued. According to a number of scholars from various schools of thought, *the Daniel 7 passage forms the prophetic backdrop of the Great Commission*, as is evident at least as early as Hippolytus (A.D. 170-236).[15] Daniel 7:13-14 reads:

> I kept looking in the night visions,
> And behold, with the clouds of heaven
> One like a Son of Man was coming,
> And He came up to the Ancient of Days
> And was presented before Him.
> And to Him was given dominion
> Glory and a kingdom,
> That all the peoples, nations, and men of every language
> Might serve Him.
> His dominion is an everlasting dominion
> Which will not pass away;
> And His kingdom is one
> Which will not be destroyed.

---

14. *Ibid.*, p. 556.

15. Hippolytus, *Treatise on Christ and Antichrist*, 26. Though he applies Dan. 7 to the future, i.e. the Second Advent. Matthew 28:18-20 "has been formulated quite consciously in terms of" Daniel 7:13-14 (Lloyd Gaston, *No Stone on Another: Studies in the Significance of the Fall of Jerusalem in the Synoptic Gospels* (Leiden: E. J. Brill, 1970), p. 385. See also the following commentators from various schools of thought: D. A. Carson, "Matthew," in Frank E. Gaebelein, ed., *The Expositor's Bible Commentary* (Grand Rapids: Zondervan, 1984), 8:595. Henry Alford, *The Greek Testament*, 4 vols., (London: 1849-1861), 1:308. Hendriksen, *Matthew*, p. 998. R. T. France, *Jesus and the Old Testament: His Application of Old Testament Passages to Himself and His Mission* (London: Tyndale, 1971), pp. 142-143. W. F. Albright and C. S. Mann, *Matthew*, in W. F. Albright and D. N. Freedman, eds., *The Anchor Bible* (Garden City, NY: Doubleday, 1971), p. 362. B. T. D. Smith, *The Gospel According to St Matthew*, in A. Nairne, ed., *The Cambridge Bible for Schools and Colleges* (Cambridge: University Press, 1933), 40:178. Frank Stagg, *Matthew-Mark*, in Clifton J. Allen, ed., *The Broadman Commentary* (Nashville: Broadman, 1969), 8:253. R. H. Fuller, "Matthew," in James L. Mays, ed., *Harper's Bible Commentary* (San Francisco: Harper and Row, 1988), p. 981. W. C. Allen, *Matthew*, in S. R. Driver, Alfred Plummer, and A. H. Briggs, eds., *The International Critical Commentary* (3rd ed.: Edinburgh: T and T Clark, 1912), 40:305. John A. Broadus, *Commentary on the Gospel of Matthew*, in Alvah Hovey, ed., *An American Commentary* (Valley Forge: Judson Press, rep. n.d. [1886]), p. 592.

Clearly this "coming" was His ascension *to heaven*: "He came *up to* the Ancient of Days." Just as clearly it was His enthronement as *king*: "to Him was given dominion." Consequently, it breathes the air of universal authority: "that *all* the peoples . . . might serve Him." Thus, it is related to the Great Commission, for the Son of Man there is given "all authority in heaven and on earth."

The Mediation of Authority

Regarding the actual implementation of the work set before the Church by our Lord, Puritan commentator Matthew Poole long ago wrote of the important function of the "go therefore" clause in the Commission: ". . . having declared his power, he delegates it."[16] In fact, "so far as earth is concerned, the dominion is only a matter of right or theory, a problem to be worked out. Hence what follows."[17] Thus, the command may be paraphrased: "All power has been given to me on earth, go ye *therefore*, and make the power a reality."[18]

The connective "therefore," standing between the declaration of "all authority" and the exhortations to "go" and "make disciples," is most appropriate and important here. It has "a peculiar force in the present connection; it draws a conclusion from the gift of all authority bestowed on Jesus. It puts all his power and his authority behind the command to evangelize the world. This shows that what otherwise would be absolutely impossible now becomes gloriously possible, yea, an assured reality."[19] The task set before this small band of men[20] would have been overwhelming were it not

---

16. Matthew Pool [sic], *Annotations Upon the Holy Bible* (New York: Robert Carter, 1856), p. 146.

17. A. B. Bruce, "The Synoptic Gospels" in Roger Nicole, ed., *Englishman's Greek Testament* (Grand Rapids: Wm. B. Eerdmans, rep. 1980 [n.d.]), 1:339.

18. *Ibid.*

19. R. C. H. Lenski, *The Interpretation of St. Matthew's Gospel* (Columbus, OH: Wartburg Press, 1943), p. 1172.

20. There is some debate as to how many are present before Christ when this Commission is given. Some commentators point to the reference to "the eleven" in verse 16. Other commentators argue that this does not preclude there being additional people present, but only specifies that all the remaining original disciples in particular were

undergirded with the universal authority claimed by Christ. Hence, the significance of the "therefore" connecting verse 18 with verse 19.

An exact literal translation of the Greek of verse 19a reads: "Going, therefore, disciple ye all the nations."[21] The "going" is a translation of a participle in the Greek. Although they express action, participles are not true verbs, but rather verbal adjectives. On a purely grammatical basis, then, participles are dependent upon main verbs for their full significance. Thus, they cannot stand alone (hence a writer's dreaded fear of the "dangling participle"!).

Some have argued from the grammar here that since the word translated "go" (literally, "going") is a participle, it may not properly be viewed as a *command* to the disciples, in that participles do not have mood.[22] They point out that if it were intended to express a *command* to go, it should have been expressed by a verb in the imperative mood. The position drawn from this grammatical argument is that Christ's command actually should be understood as: "Wherever you happen to be, make disciples."

Of course it is true that "wherever" we "happen to be" it is incumbent upon us to make disciples. Nevertheless, grammatically a participle can carry the force of the main verb's action. This is because the participle is so closely tied to the main verb that it partakes in sense the verb's force. And the participle here contextually does have the imperative *force* of the main verb, despite its not having the imperative *form*.[23]

---

present. It is often asserted that the appearance of Christ to the 500 brethren (1 Cor. 15:6) must have been at this time because of (1) the difficulty of placing that appearance elsewhere and (2) the difficulty of explaining the "doubt" expressed by some present, if only the eleven were present (Matt. 28:17). For example, A. T. Robertson, *Word Pictures in the New Testament*, 6 vols., (Nashville: Broadman, 1930), 1:244. Nevertheless, the point remains: the number was small in comparison to the task.

21. Alfred Marshall, *The Interlinear Greek-English New Testament* (2nd ed: Grand Rapids: Zondervan, 1959), p. 136.

22. Robert O. Culver, "What Is the Church's Commission?", *Bibliotheca Sacra* 125 [1968] 239-253.

23. See: William Hendriksen, *The Gospel of Matthew* (*New Testament Commentary*) (Grand Rapids: Baker, 1973), p. 999; Cleon Rogers, "The Great Commission," *Bibliotheca Sacra* 130 [1973] 258-267.

Furthermore, that this is actually a *command* to "go" may be seen in the history of the early church contained in Acts. There we witness the "going" of the disciples into the world. In addition, the related commissions of Christ, which urge the progression of the gospel from Jerusalem outward to all the world, evidence the outward reaching, militant expansion of Christ's concern, and suggest that understanding for Matthew 28:19.[24]

The point, when all is said and done, is that Christ expected His New Covenant people to *go*, that is, to be militant in their promotion of the true faith. Under the Old Covenant, Israel as a nation was confined to a land with well-defined parameters.[25] She was to exercise her influence among the nations from *within that land* and *by example* as she remained "in the midst of the land" (Deut. 4:5-8).[26] Never is she authorized by God to conquer nations outside of her borders for purposes of annexation.[27] In fact, rather than her going to the nations,

---

24. Luke 24:47; Mark 16:15-20; Acts 1:8. Jerome (A.D. 340-420) wrote of Jerusalem: "It would be tedious to inumerate all the prophets and holy men who have been sent forth from this place." Jerome, Letter 46 *To Marcella*.

25. Gen. 15:18; Exo. 23:31; Num. 34:3-12; Deut. 11:31; Josh. 1:4; I Kgs. 4:20-21. This specific land was taken from the Canaanites and given to Israel on the basis of divine sanctions of God's Law against the horrible perversity of the Canaanites in their breaking of God's Law (Lev. 18:24-30).

26. See 1 Kgs. 5:7; Psa. 2:10-11; 119:45; Isa. 51:4. On Deut. 4:5-8 Ridderbos comments: "The purpose of his instruction is for Israel to keep these laws when they have entered Canaan. Observing these decrees and laws will show Israel's wisdom and understanding in the eyes of the nations. The phrase 'great nation' reflects the respect the nations will have for Israel for this reason. Israel's missionary task vis-a-vis the pagan world is indicated in a veiled manner: This respect for Israel implies respect for Him from whom Israel received these laws. This missionary task is later further unfolded in prophecy, especially where Israel is prophetically described as the servant of the Lord, His messenger whom He sends (Isa. 42:19) to proclaim His praise (43:21), who is called to be His witness (43:10), in whose mouth He has put His words (51:16)." J. Ridderbos, *Deuteronomy* (*Bible Student's Commentary*) (Grand Rapids: Regency Reference Library, 1984), p. 83.

27. In regard to this we should note: (1) Israel's king was forbidden to "multiply horses" (Deut. 17:16), apparently due to the fact that in Israel's rugged terrain horses would only be profitable to a king determined to expand his borders and to project military power into foreign lands. (2) God establishes in His law protections that preserve the integrity of landmarks (Deut. 19:14; 27:17; Prov. 22:28; 23:10). (3) A prophetic judgment on Ammon for attempting "to enlarge their borders" is discovered in (Amos 1:13). (4) Prophetic visions warn of God's wrath against nations bent on imperial

the nations were to come to her.[28]

Now, with the transformation of the Church into her New Covenant phase[29] and her development from immaturity to maturity (Gal. 3:23-26), militancy characterizes her energies. She is to go forth into all the world sowing seed, unshackled by geographic considerations.[30] For a very important purpose the Church is "in the world" (John 17:15): to go forth with kingly authority to confront the nations with the demands of God. Thus, the Commission makes reference to His authority over "the earth" (v. 18b) and our obligation to enforce that authority over "the nations" (v. 19a).

The Great Commission sends down from above an *obligation* upon God's people. It can no more be reduced to "The Good Idea" than the Ten Commandments can be deemed the "Ten Suggestions." It is not an option for the people of God. It is an obligatory task laid upon those who are not only created in the image of God (as all men are[31]), but who are ethically renewed in that image by the saving mercies of Christ.[32] It is an obligation that is laid upon His people who dwell on the earth here and now, for "the earth is the Lord's and the fullness thereof."[33]

Through hierarchical covenantal arrangement, we are under *obligation* to inform the people of the world of the ownership of all things by the Lord God and of the authority of His Son over

---

annexation (Dan. 2; 7). In light of all this, the law in Deut. 20:10-11 (regarding war against nations beyond Israel) seems to have in mind warfare "on a just occasion," i.e. defensive war; see: Robert Jamieson, A. R. Faussett, David Brown, 2 vols., *A Commentary, Critical and Explanatory on the Old and New Testaments* (Hartford: S. S. Scranton, n.d.), 1:134.

28. E.g., 1 Kgs. 10; 2 Chron. 9. See the imagery involved in the Messianic prophecies which portray the world as coming to Jerusalem, Isa. 2:3; Mic. 4:2; Zech. 8:2.

29. The New Covenant has to do with the Church: Jer. 31:31-34; Matt. 26:28; Mark 14:24; Luke 22:20; 1 Cor. 11:25; 2 Cor. 3:6; Heb. 7:22; 8:6-13; 9:15-16; 12:24.

30. Cf. Matt. 13:1-52; Matt. 28:19; Mark 16:15; Luke 24:47; Acts 1:8; 13:47.

31. Gen. 1:26-27; 5:1,3; 9:6; 1 Cor. 11:7; Jas. 3:9. Although the word "image" is absent, the idea is also contained in Psalm 8 and Acts 17:28.

32. Rom. 8:29; Col. 3:10; Eph. 4:24.

33. This glorious statement is repeated time and again throughout Scripture. For example see: Exo. 9:29; 19:5; Lev. 25:23; Deut. 10:14; 1 Sam. 2:8; 2 Chron. 29:11, 14; Job 41:11; Psa. 24:1; 50:12; 89:11; Psa. 115:16; 1 Cor. 10:26, 28.

all. We are to proclaim that redemption is necessary for acceptance by God and salvation from eternal judgment. We are to instruct men of their consequent responsibility to serve God in all of life that results from such glorious redemption.

The Extension of Authority

According to its very words, the mission of the Commission is what truly may be called *great*. Christ commands: "Go therefore and make disciples of all the *nations*." But what does this mean? The significance of the word "nations" is of serious consequence. Its apprehension has become a point of dispute in the recent debate among evangelicals.[34]

Because of what we noted above, we must see the hierarchical obligation of the Great Commission in its command to "*Go* . . . make disciples of all nations." This command is remarkable here because of its contrast to Christ's earlier command, "*Do not go* in the way of the Gentiles."[35] The gospel of salvation was initially "to the Jew first,"[36] so it was necessary that it *begin* its work and influence in Jerusalem.[37]

But Matthew's record of the appearance of the non-Jewish Magi from the East (Matt. 2:1-2), His teaching regarding the coming into the kingdom of people from the east and the west (Matt. 8:11), the kingdom parables involving the world (Matt. 13), and so forth, make it clear that *Christ's ministry always expected the eventual inclusion of the non-Jewish nations*. This was not some new and unexpected program shift, for even the Old Testament held forth the promise of the salvation of non-Jews.[38] In fact, the apostles frequently cited the Old Testament

---

34. See: Hal Lindsey, *The Road to Holocaust* (New York: Bantam, 1989), pp. 49, 277; Dave Hunt, *Whatever Happened to Heaven?* (Eugene, OR: Harvest, 1988), pp. 231-235; H. Wayne House and Thomas D. Ice, *Dominion Theology: Blessing or Curse?* (Portland, OR: Multnomah, 1988), pp. 150-161; Albert James Dager, "Kingdom Theology: Part III, " *Media Spotlight* (January-June, 1987), p. 11.
35. Matt. 10:5-6; cp. Matt. 15:24.
36. Rom. 1:16; 2:10; John 4:22.
37. Luke 24:47; Acts 1:8; 3:26.
38. Gen. 12:3; 22:18; Psa. 22:27; 86:9; Isa. 5:26; 45:22; 49:6; 60:1-3; Jer. 16:19; Mic. 4:2; Zech. 8:22-23 Mal. 1:11.

prophecies in defense of their reaching out to the Gentiles.[39]

But some evangelicals tend to understand the command to mean nothing more than: "in spreading the gospel, no part of the world is to be omitted."[40] Consequently, it merely means that "the purpose of the church in this present age [is] that of a witness."[41] The Great Commission is said to involve the salvation of "individuals" from among the nations, because "making a disciple in the Biblical sense is an individual thing."[42]

Who among us would disagree with these statements — as far as they go? Surely Christ's words, "Go therefore and make disciples of all the nations" cannot mean less than that the gospel is a universal gospel to be proclaimed to people in all nations. And just as surely is it held by all evangelicals that the Great Commission demands the salvation of individual sinners from their own sins.

But is this all that it entails? Does the Great Commission merely seek the proclamation of the gospel to all nations? That is, does it only seek the salvation of scattered individuals from throughout the world? Or is there more here than we may have supposed?

Christ's command is to make disciples of all the "nations." The Greek word translated "nations" here is ethne (the plural of ethnos), which is an interesting word that serves a vital function in the Great Commission. Let us consider the word meaning itself, then note how it is more appropriate for the Great Commission than any other similar words might have been.

The Meaning of *Ethnos*

1. *Its Etymological Derivation*. The word *ethnos* was common in the Greek language from ancient times. It is widely agreed

---

39. Acts 13:47; 15:15-17; Rom. 4:17; 9:24-26; 15:10-12; Gal. 3:8.
40. Howard Vos, *Mark*, p. 141.
41. House and Ice, *Dominion Theology*, p. 165. See also: Anthony A. Hoekema, *The Bible and the Future* (Grand Rapids: Wm. B. Eerdmans, 1979), p. 138.
42. Lindsey, *Road to Holocaust*, p. 277. In another context, J. D. Pentecost is aware of the precariousness of the dispensationalist individualization of the term "*ethnos*" and attempts an argument supportive of it (Pentecost, *Things to Come*, p. 421).

among etymologists that it was derived from another Greek word, *ethos*, which means "'mass' or 'host' or 'multitude' bound by the same manners, customs and other distinctive features"[43] and was ultimately derived from the Sanskrit *svadha*, which means "own state, habit."[44] Therefore, *ethos* contemplates "a body of people living according to one custom and rule."[45] In fact, *ethos* itself is found in the New Testament and means "habit, custom" (Luke 22:39; Acts 25:16).

Returning to the specific word found in the Great Commission, Greek lexicographer Joseph Thayer lists five nuances of the term *ethnos*: (1) A "multitude . . . associated or living together." (2) "A multitude of individuals of the same nature or genus." (3) "Race, nation." (4) "Foreign nations not worshipping the true God; pagans, Gentiles." (5) "Gentile Christians."[46] Consequently, the word *ethnos* speaks not so much of stray individuals as such, but of *collected masses* of individuals *united together* by a common bond, as in a culture, society, or nation.

2. *Its New Testament Usage.* The root idea of the word *ethnos* is easily discernible in Acts 17:26: "And He made from one, every *nation* of mankind to live on all the face of the earth." In

43. Karl Ludwig Schmidt, "*ethnos*" in Gerhard Kittle, ed., *Theological Dictionary of the New Testament*, 10 vols., trans. by Geoffery W. Bromiley (Grand Rapids: Wm. B. Eerdmans, 1964), 2:369. See also: Ernest Klein, *A Comprehensive Etymological Dictionary of the English Language* (New York: Elsevier, 1966), 1:547.
44. Robert K. Barnhart, *The Barnhart Dictionary of Etymology* (Bronx, NY: H. W. Wilson, 1988), p. 345. See also: Carl Darling Buck, *A Dictionary of Selected Synonyms in the Principal Indo-European Languages* (Chicago: University of Chicago Press, 1949), entry 19.22, p. 1315. The Old Testament Hebrew, which is translated in the Greek Septuagint version of the Old Testament by *ethne*, is *goi*, which is used "in the primary sense of a connected body" (J. A. Selbie, "Gentiles" in James Hastings, ed., *A Dictionary of the Bible Dealing with its Language, Literature, and Contents Including the Biblical Theology* (Edinburgh: T and T Clark, rep. 1955 [1899]), 2:149. This Hebrew word means "flow together, as a crowd, and was originally used in a general sense of any nation" (John M'Clintock and James Strong, *Cyclopaedia of Biblical, Theological, and Ecclesiastical Literature* (Grand Rapids: Baker, rep. 1969 [1887]), 3:788.
45. Richard Chenevix Trench, *Synonyms of the New Testament* (9th ed.: Grand Rapids: Wm. B. Eerdmans, 1969 [1880]), p. 368. The word is "based on such notions as . . . common 'birth', 'customs', or 'language', or are words for 'country' used also for its 'people'." Buck, *Dictionary*, Entry 19.22, p. 1315.
46. Joseph Henry Thayer, *A Greek-English Lexicon of the New Testament* (New York: American Book Co., 1889), p. 168.

addition, the same is true of Revelation 7:9, where a multitude of saints is gathered "from every *nation* and all tribes and peoples and tongues." As a matter of fact, the national-cultural-collective significance of the word is pointed to by the use of *ethnos* in a number of places outside of Matthew in the New Testament.[47] The Jews as a distinct culture and national entity are even called an *ethnos* in the New Testament in many places,[48] showing the term does not necessarily mean "gentile" in the sense of "non-Jew."[49]

In fact, the term *ethnos*, when applied by Jews to others, is for the very purpose of distinguishing the national culture (including religion, tradition, manners, etc.) of non-Jewish peoples from Jewish national culture.[50] As such, it involves the collective or corporate idea of a people's culture and is not tied merely to stray individuals. In addition, in the form found in Matthew 28:19, the phrase "all the nations" is also found in several other verses. In those verses it speaks of national units or whole cultures, as such.[51]

3. *Its Matthaen Function.* Interestingly, a study of Matthew's own employment of the term *ethnos* provides statistical evidence in our favor. In Matthew, nine out of fourteen appearances of the term (or 71% of its occurrences) are used in a way clearly referring to *nations as such*: Matthew 4:15; 10:18[52]; 12:18,

---

47. According to Arndt-Gingrich, p. 217, these verses include: Mark 10:42; 11:17; 13:8, 10; Luke 12:30; 21:10; 22:25; Acts 8:9; 9:15; 10:35; 13:19; 17:26. Also see: Josephus, *Antiquities of the Jews* 11:215; 12:6, 135; 18:25; Hermas, *Similitudes* 9:17:2; Barnabas 13:2; Philo, *Decalouge* 96; 1 Clement 59:4; 2 Clement 13:2.

48. See: Luke 7:5; 23:2; John 11:48-52; 18:35; Acts 10:22; 24:2, 10, 17; 26:4; 28:19.

49. The very term "gentile" in English is even derived from the Latin *gentilis, gens,* which means "nation" or "tribe." See: *The Compact Edition of the Oxford English Dictionary,* 2 Vols., (Oxford: Oxford University Press, 1971), 1:1130.

50. Interestingly, rather than *ethnos,* the New Testament most often employs the Greek word *hellenes* ("Greek") when distinguishing the Jew from others. See: John 7:35; 12:20; Acts 6:1; 9:29; 11:20; 14:1; 16:1, 3; 17:4, 12; 18:5; 19:10, 17; 20:21; 20:21; 21:28; Rom. 1:14, 16; 2:9, 10; 3:9; 10:12; 1 Cor. 1:22, 24; 10:32; 12:13; Gal. 2:3; 3:28; Col. 3:11.

51. Matt. 24:14; 25:32(?); Mark 11:17; Luke 21:24; 24:47; Rom. 16:26; Gal. 3:8; Rev. 12:5; 14:8; 15:4; 18:3, 23. Even amillennialist theologian Anthony A. Hoekema admits "nations" in Matthew 28:19 refers to collected peoples on the various continents, although he reduces the meaning of the Commission to a mere witness. See: Anthony Hoekema, *The Bible and the Future* (Grand Rapids: Wm. B. Eerdmans, 1979), p. 139.

52. Note the contextual reference to governors and kings. Also compare this

21^{53}; 20:25; $21:43^{54}$; 24:7, 9, 14. In two other instances (or 14%), the term is probably to be understood as betokening "nation": Matt. $6:32,^{55}$ and $25:32.^{56}$ The two instances (or 14%) that probably involve the generalistic conception "gentiles" or "people"[57] are Matt. 10:5 and 20:19. The remaining instance is found in the text under discussion, Matthew 28:19. In point of fact, it should be noted, virtually all major English translations render the term in the Great Commission with the English "nations," rather than "gentiles."[58]

Lenski clearly applies the plural *ta ethne* of Matthew 28:19 to nations, when he argues for infant baptism from the passage on the basis of there being children who composed "such a large part of every nation."[59] Lange holds the same view, when he comments on the phrase: "nations, as nations, are to be Christianized."[60] In their *Lexicon*, Arndt and Gingrich provide two entries in explication of the term *ethnos*: (1) "nation, people" and (2) "heathen, pagans, Gentiles." Under the first listing they place Matthew 28:19.[61]

The Significance of *Ethnos*

It would seem that the term *ethnos*, which Christ employed

---

prophecy with the Acts record of persecution.

53. The Old Testament reading is from Isa. 42:1-3, where the NASV has "nations." That text speaks of "justice" (Isa. 42:1, 3, 4), a concern for national entities.

54. Here a contrast is set up between unfaithful Israel and the New Testament phase Church, as if comparing two nations.

55. Notice the setting, which contrasts *ethnos* to "the *kingdom* of God" (Matt. 6:33). Besides, surely Israel would be included among those who seek food and clothing (Matt. 6:31-32), rather than just non-Jews ("gentiles").

56. Even some dispensationalists argue for this reference to refer to distinct political entities (A. C. Gaebelein, *Matthew*, 2:247). The word is translated "nation" in the following versions: NASV, NIV, NEB, NKJV, RSV, ASV, Moffatt, Williams, Beck, and Phillips.

57. As in the *Today's English Version* (TEV).

58. See: KJV, NASV, NIV, NKJV, RSV, Williams, Moffatt, Weymouth, Phillips, and Amplified.

59. Lenski, *Matthew*, pp. 1178-1179.

60. Lange, *Matthew*, p. 557.

61. W. F. Arndt and F. W. Gingrich, *A Greek-English Lexicon of the New Testament and Other Early Christian Literature* (Chicago: University of Chicago, 1957), p. 217.

in the Great Commission, carries with it an important significance. He calls His followers to "make disciples of all the nations." He does not merely say "disciple all *men*" (although this lesser point is true also). In that case he would have chosen the Greek word *anthropos*, which would allow the reference to indicate men as individual humans, rather than as collected races, cultures, societies, or nations. Neither does He call for the discipling of "all *kingdoms*" (*basileia*), as if He laid claim only to political authority. Rather, He calls for the discipling of "all the *nations*" (*ethnos*), involving men as individuals united together in all their socio-cultural labors and relations.

The discipling work of the Great Commission, then, aims at the comprehensive application of Christ's authority over men through conversion. *As the numbers of converts increase, this providentially leads to the subsuming under the authority of Christ whole institutions, cultures, societies, and governments.* As Matthew Henry put it centuries ago: "Christianity should be twisted in with national constitutions, . . . the kingdoms of the world should become Christ's kingdoms, and their kings the church's nursing fathers. . . . [D]o your utmost to make the nations Christian nations. . . . Christ the Mediator is setting up a kingdom in the world, bring the nations to be his subjects."[62]

The Goal of Authority

This understanding of the hierarchical administration of the sovereignty of the Great Commission helps us understand

---

62. Matthew Henry, *Matthew Henry's Commentary on the Whole Bible* (Old Tappan, NJ: Fleming H. Revell n.d. [1721]), 5:446. It must be observed that Henry says: *Christianity*, not the institutional Church, should be twisted in with national constitutions. The best modern treatment of this doctrine is found in North, *Political Polytheism, op. cit.* Contrary to some, not even the Mosaic Law endorses a *merging* or *union* of Church and State. It directs, rather, a *harmony* and *mutual respect* of Church and State under God. Even in Old Testament Israel there was a strong distinction between Church and State. There was a clear separation of priest and king; there was a difference between temple and palace. Israel was organized as a *nation* under Moses. Moses was Israel's civil ruler; Aaron, not Moses, was the father of the priestly line. That God kept the ecclesiastical and civil offices separate in Israel is clear from such passages as 1 Sam. 13:11-13, 2 Chron. 19:5-11 and 2 Chron. 26:16-21. Consequently, McClain is quite mistaken, when he asserts: "Under the Mosaic law religious and civil authority were one. There was no separation of church and state." Alva J. McClain, *Law and Grace* (Chicago: Moody, 1954), p. 14.

certain of the universalistic sounding passages that speak of redemption. Christ saves individuals, to be sure. Praise God for that glorious truth — I myself am an individual! But His plan and goal is to save *masses* of individuals and the *cultures* that arise from their labors, as well. His plan is one of comprehensive salvation. This may be noted in certain universalistic passages. Although we are prone to speak of Christ as "my personal Savior," we too often overlook the fact He is also declared to be "the Savior of the *world*." There are several passages which speak of the world-wide scope of redemption.

Cosmic Salvation

In John 1:29, John the Baptist sees Jesus and utters these words: "Behold, the Lamb of God who takes away the sin of the *world*." In 1 John 4:14 we read: "The Father has sent the Son to be the Savior of the *world*." John 3:16-17 says "God so loved the *world* that He gave His only begotten Son, that whoever believes in Him should not perish, but have eternal life. For God did not send the Son into the world to judge the world; but that the *world* should be saved through Him" (cp. John 12:47). 1 John 2:2 teaches that "He Himself is the propitiation for our sins; and not for ours only, but also for those of the whole *world*." In 2 Corinthians 5:19 Paul conceives of Christ's active labor thus: "God was in Christ reconciling the *world* to Himself."

Now these passages clearly present Christ in His redemptive labors. In them we learn that: He is called the *Lamb* of God; He *takes away sin*; His purpose in coming was to *save*; He provides *propitiation* for the sinner; He is *reconciling sinners* to Himself.

But what does the Greek word *kosmos* (translated "world") mean in these passages that speak of the scope of redemption? This noun originally had to do with a building erected from individual parts to form a whole. It came to be applied to relations between men, as in the case of ordering soldiers in armies and governments in matters of state. Eventually *kosmos* came to speak of the well ordered universe, and was an important term in Greek philosophy.

In the New Testament the word *kosmos* spoke of the sum of all created being, including both the animate and inanimate creation. Acts 17:24 speaks of God creating the "world and all that is in it." God created an orderly creation, as is evident from Genesis 1. Hence, He created a *kosmos*.

The word "world" as employed in the preceding passages regarding world salvation refer, then, to *the world as the orderly system of men and things*. That is, the world that God created and loves is His creation as He intended it: a world in subjection to man who in turn is to be in subjection to God (Psa. 8).

A point frequently overlooked in the passages cited above is that those verses clearly speak of the world-system focus of His sovereign redemption. Thus, in each of the passages passing under our scrutiny, we have reference to the aim of full and free salvation for the *kosmos*, the world as a system. That is, Christ's redemptive labors are designed to redeem the created order of men and things. Hence, the Great Commission command to disciple "all nations" involves not only all men as men (*anthropos*), but all men in their cultural connections (*ethnos*) (Matt. 28:19), for Christ "is Lord of all" (Acts 10:36). All of society is to be subdued by the gospel of the sovereign Christ.

Consequently, as A. T. Robertson marvelled regarding the Great Commission: "It is the sublimest of all spectacles to see the Risen Christ without money or army or state charging this band of five hundred men and women with world conquest and bring them to believe it possible and to undertake it with serious passion and power."[63] Yet that is precisely what Christ did. As Chamblin put it, when speaking of the giving of such authority to Christ: "God the Father . . . now wills that Jesus' existent authority (7:29; 8:9) be exercised universally."[64]

Cultural Redemption

Salvation is designed for the "world as a system" (*kosmos*)

63. A. T. Robertson, *Word Pictures in the New Testament* (Nashville: Broadman, 1930), 1:244-245.
64. Chamblin, *Matthew*, p. 760.

involving men in their cultural relations (*ethnos*). Obviously, then, it must follow that its effects should be pressed in every aspect of life and culture, not just in the inner-personal realm.[65] In fact, Christ's Commission claims just that in two very important phrases.

(1) When Christ lays claim to "all authority," He is specifying the comprehensiveness of His authority. Christ here claims "every form of authority [and] command of all means necessary for the advancement of the kingdom of God."[66] Or, to put it another way, He claims "unlimited authority in every area."[67] *No* form of authority escapes His sovereign grant.

(2) When He adds *"in heaven and on earth,"* He is specifying the realm of the exercise His authority. He is claiming His authority is equally intense on earth as it is in heaven. In other words, the authority He holds in heaven over the affairs of its redeemed residents and the holy angels is held in the affairs of earth over men, as well. Jesus Christ was given *"all authority in heaven. . .* so that he can make use of all the resources of heaven [and] *all authority upon earth . . .* so that he can turn every institution and power and person on earth to account."[68]

Truly Christ is claiming unlimited authority over *every* realm. He is not claiming it solely over the limited realms of the inner-personal life, or over a few select realms, such as the family, or the Church. This is made quite clear in various pregnant expressions applied to Him later in the New Testament. Philippians 2:9-11 contains a strong statement in this regard:

Therefore God *highly exalted*[69] Him, and bestowed on Him the

---

65. Gary North, "Comprehensive Redemption: A Theology for Social Action" (1981), in North, *Is the World Running Down? Crisis in the Christian Worldview* (Tyler, Texas: Institute for Christian Economics, 1988), Appendix C.

66. A. B. Bruce, "Matthew," in W. Robertson Nicoll, ed., *Englishman's Greek Testament* (Grand Rapids: Wm. B. Eerdmans, rep. 1980 [n.d.]), 1:339. See also: Hendriksen, *Matthew*, p. 998.

67. Cleon Rogers, "The Great Commission" in *Bibliotheca Sacra* 130 (Jul-Sept, 1973), 265.

68. James Morison, *Commentary on the Gospel According to Matthew* (London: Hamilton, Adams, 1870), p. 679.

69. "In the present passage a verb is used which in the New Testament occurs only

name which is *above every name*, that at the name of Jesus *every* knee should bow, of those who are in heaven, and *on earth*, and under the earth, and that *every* tongue should confess that Jesus Christ is *Lord* to the glory of God the Father. (Emphasis added)

This corresponds well with what is written in Ephesians 1:20-22:

He raised Him from the dead, and seated Him *at His right hand* in the heavenly places, *far above all rule and authority and power and dominion and every name that is named*, not only in this age, but also in the one to come. And He *put all things in subjection* under His feet, and gave Him as *head over all things* to the church. (Emphasis added)

These passages are supplemented by several other verses,[70] as well as the Revelation statement that He is "Lord of lords and King of kings."[71]

Regarding the civil-political area of man's culture, which is perhaps the stickiest aspect of the question, this explains why kings are obligated to rule by Him,[72] under Him,[73] and as His "ministers" to promote His Law,[74] according to the glorious gospel of the blessed God.[75] The earthly political authority to which Satan arrogantly laid claim, by which he oppressed the nations, and which he offered to Christ[76] was righteously won by Christ's glorious redemptive labor.

His "all authority" over "all the nations" demands we preach His crown rights over all men and all their institutions,

---

in this *one* instance and is here applied only to *him*, namely, the very "*super*-exalted." William Hendriksen, *Philippians* (*New Testament Commentary*) (Grand Rapids: Baker, 1962), p. 113. Compare Acts 2:33; 5:31; Heb. 7:26; Eph. 4:10.

70. For example: Col. 2:10; Rom. 14:9, 12; 1 Cor. 15:27; Heb. 1:4; and 1 Pet. 3:22.

71. Rev. 17:14; 19:16.

72. 2 Chron. 20:6; Prov. 8:15; Luke 18:8.

73. Psa. 2:10-12; Psa. 47:2, 7, 8; 72:8-11; 148:11; Dan. 4:1, 25-27, 37; 6:25ff; Acts 17:7; Rev. 1:5.

74. Rom. 13:4, 6. Other religious titles are applied to civil rulers, such as "servant" and "anointed." See: Isa. 44:28; 45:1; Jer. 25:9; 27:6; 43:10.

75. Rom. 13:4-9; 1 Tim. 1:8-11.

76. Matt. 4:8-9; Luke 4:5,6.

cultures, societies, and nations. The saving of multitudes of individuals *must* eventually lead to cultural Christianization under Christ's rule and to His glory by His providence, in conformity with God's creational purpose. This world order was designed to have man set over it, to the glory of God.[77] This is why at the very beginning of human history unfallen man was a cultural creature.[78]

The salvation wrought by the implementation of the Great Commission does not merely involve a static entry into the Lamb's Book of Life; it involves also a life-transforming change within the center of man's being.[79] That is, it is not just something *entered* in the *record book* of heaven in order to change man's *status* (legal justification based on the finished work of Christ).[80] Certainly it involves that, but there is more. It also involves something *effected* on earth *in man* to change his *character* (spiritual sanctification generated by the continuing work of the Holy Spirit).[81]

Christ's saving work sovereignly overwhelms man and effects in him a "new birth,"[82] thereby making the believer a "new creature"[83] or a "new man,"[84] creating in him a new

---

77. Gen. 1:26-28; 9:2; Job 35:11; Psa. 8; 115:16; Heb. 2:6-8.
78. See earlier discussion in Chapter 1.
79. It is important to recognize that the recently renewed debate called the Lordship Controversy indicates anew that the some evangelicals neither understand properly the nature of eschatology (the outworking of cosmic redemption) nor the nature of soteriology (the outworking of personal redemption). The anti-Lordship view advocated by certain evangelicals, such as Charles Ryrie and Zane Hodges, does not adequately take into account the genuine, Holy Spirit-effected change wrought in the elect sinner's heart at the moment of the new birth. See Charles C. Ryrie, *So Great Salvation* (Wheaton, IL: Victor, 1990) and Zane C. Hodges, *Absolutely Free!* (Grand Rapids: Zondervan, 1989). For a more biblical understanding, see: Kenneth L. Gentry, Jr., "The Great Option: A Study of the Lordship Controversy" in *Baptist Reformation Review*, 5:1 (Spring, 1976) 49-79; John F. MacArthur, Jr., *The Gospel According to Jesus* (Grand Rapids: Zondervan, 1988); and John Murray, *The Epistle to the Romans* (New International Commentary on the New Testament) (Grand Rapids: Wm. B. Eerdmans, 1959 [rep. 1968]), pp. 211-238.
80. Rom. 4:25; 5:1,9; 1 Cor. 6:11; Gal. 2:16; 3:24; Tit. 3:7.
81. Rom. 6:3-14; 8:10, 14; Eph. 2:10; Phil. 1:6; 2:13; 1 Thess. 5:23-24; 2 Thess. 2:13; Tit. 3:5; 1 Pet. 1:2.
82. John 1:13; 3:3; 1 Cor. 4:15; Tit. 3:5; Jms. 1:18; 1 Pet. 1:3, 23; 1 John 2:29.
83. 2 Cor. 5:17; Gal. 6:15; Eph. 2:10.
84. Eph. 4:22-24; Col. 3:9-10.

character[85] in that he has been resurrected and made alive from spiritual death.[86] It brings him "all spiritual blessings,"[87] puts him under the power of grace,[88] insures the indwelling of the Holy Spirit[89] and of Christ,[90] which imparts the power of God within,[91] and secures the intercession of Christ in his behalf.[92]

All of this *must* lead to confrontation with and the altering of non-Christian culture, for Paul commands: "work out your salvation with fear and trembling, for it is God who is at work in you, both to will and to work for His good pleasure" (Phil. 2:12-13). Paul is not saying we are to "work *for* our salvation" (as if guilty sinners could merit God's favor!), but that the salvation we possess must be "worked out" into every area of our lives. In short, we are to work out the salvation that is now ours. Consequently, we are driven by divine obligation and salvific duty to "expose the works of darkness" (Eph. 5:11) by being "the salt of the earth" and "the light of the world" (Matt. 5:13, 14). Salvation, then, exercises a gradualistic, dynamic and transforming influence in the life of the individual convert to Christ. This is *progressive sanctification*. But this process is not limited to a hypothetical, exclusively personal realm of ethics. As salvation spreads to others, it also establishes a motivated, energetic *kingdom* of the faithful who are organized to operate as "a nation producing the fruit of" the kingdom.[93]

Thus, in 2 Corinthians 10:4-5 we read:

> For the weapons of our warfare are not of the flesh, but divinely powerful for the destruction of fortresses. We are destroying speculations and every lofty thing raised up against the knowledge

---

85. Jer. 31:33; Eze. 11:19; 36:26; Rom. 7:6; 2 Cor. 3:3; Heb. 8:10; 10:16.
86. John 3:36; 5:21, 24; 6:67; Rom. 6:4-9; Eph. 2:1,5; Col. 2:12,13; 3:1; 1 John 5:11.
87. Rom. 8:32; 1 Cor. 3:21; Eph. 1:3; 2 Pet. 1:3.
88. Rom. 6:14; 7:5,6; Eph. 1:19; 1 John 5:18.
89. Rom. 8:9-11; 1 Cor. 3:16; 6:19; 2 Cor. 6:16; Gal. 4:6; Eph. 2:22; 2 Tim. 1:14; 1 John 4:13.
90. Rom. 8:10; Gal. 2:20; Phil. 1:19.
91. 1 Cor. 12:6; Eph. 1:19; Phil. 2:12-13; Tit. 3:5; 1 John 5:4-5.
92. Rom. 8:34; Heb. 7:25; 9:24; 1 John 2:1.
93. Matt. 21:43; cp. 1 Pet. 2:9; Rev. 1:6.

of God, and we are taking every thought captive to the obedience of Christ.

The One who claims "all authority in heaven and on earth" and who has been given "a name above every name that is named" is He who has commissioned us to destroy *"every* lofty thing raised up against the knowledge of God" and to take *"every* thought captive to the obedience of Christ" — not *some* thoughts or *inner-personal* thoughts only. This is to be done imperceptibly from within,[94] not by armed revolution from without,[95] as we "do business" until He comes (Luke 19:13).

There is another angle from which we may expect the culture transforming effect of redemption: the negative angle, *the correction of sin.* As poetically put in the great Christmas hymn "Joy to the World":

No more let sins and sorrows grow,
Nor thorns infest the ground;
He comes to make His blessings flow
Far as the curse is found.

The salvation that Christ brings is salvation *from sin.* His redemption is designed to flow "far as the curse is found." The angel who appeared to Joseph instructed him, "You shall call His name Jesus, for it is He who will save His people from their sins" (Matt. 1:21b).

Now, then, how far is the curse of sin found? How wide ranging is sin? *The curse of sin is found everywhere throughout the world! It permeates and distorts every area of man's life!* For this reason Christ's Commission to His Church, as recorded in Luke 24:47 (and implied in Matt. 28:19-20), reads: "Thus it is written, that the Christ should suffer and rise again from the death the third day; and that repentance for forgiveness of sins

---

94. Matt. 13:33; Luke 17:21. "The primary need, today as always, is the need for widespread personal repentance before God. We therefore need a Holy Spirit-initiated Christian revival to extend the kingdom of God across the face of the earth." North, *Political Polytheism*, p. 611 (see also pp. 133,157, 585-6).

95. Zech. 4:6; Matt. 26:51-52; John 18:36-37; 2 Cor. 10:4-5.

should be proclaimed in His name to all the nations, beginning from Jerusalem." Again we are confronted with salvation — here via repentance from sin — for "all the nations."

If man is totally depraved,[96] then that depravity extends to and accounts for the pervasive corruption of all of man's cultural activities. Instead of the "Midas Touch," fallen man has the "Minus Touch." The sinner's touch reduces the quality, value, and effectiveness of everything he does, compared to what he would do were he sinless. Surely salvation from sin involves salvation from all the implications of sin, including institutional, cultural, social, and political sins. And just as surely, the Christian should authoritatively confront sinful conduct and labor toward its replacement with the righteous alternative.

Incredibly, one best-selling evangelical author has even castigated John the Baptist because of his preaching against the sin of the political authority in his realm, King Herod Antipas!

> John the Baptist rebuked Herod Antipas for taking his half-brother Philip's wife. . . . Could it be that John, who was imprisoned and later beheaded by Herod because of this reproof, may have needlessly cut his ministry to Israel short by aiming his remarks at the wrong target?[97]

This mistaken argument logically would lead to a rebuke of Christ Himself for calling the same Herod a "fox" (Luke 13:32)! Could it be that Jesus "needlessly cut his ministry to Israel short by aiming his remarks at the wrong target"? Surely not!

Conclusion

We have seen that the Great Commission directs Christians to pursue the promotion of Christ's sovereign rule over men

---

96. "Total depravity" indicates man is sin-infected in every aspect of his being, including his will, emotions, intellect, strength, etc. See: Gen. 6:5; 8:21; Eccl. 9:3; Jer. 17:9; Mark 7:21-23; John 3:19; Rom. 8:7,8; 1 Cor. 2:14; Eph. 4:17-19; 5:8; Tit. 3:5. Man is "dead in trespasses and sin;" he is not sick (Eph. 2:1, 5; cp. John 5:24; Rom. 6:13; Col. 2:13).

97. Hunt, *Whatever Happened to Heaven?*, p. 82.

through salvation. Indeed, it directs our labors to redeeming not only individuals, but the whole lives of individuals, which generate their culture. Christ avoided terms that easily could have been given a lesser significance, when He commanded His followers to "disciple all *nations.*" And He insured that we understand the Commission properly by undergirding it with the redemptive reality of His possessing "all authority in heaven and on earth." (I will return to this theme to emphasize the prospect of its victory in Chapter 7, where I will consider Covenantal Succession.)

Herschell Hobbs has preserved for us an insightful comment most apropos to our study: "Dr. Gaines S. Dobbins was asked, 'But is not conversion the end of salvation?' He replied, 'Yes, but which end?'"[98] That is the question before us.

---

98. Herschell H. Hobbs, *An Exposition of the Gospel of Matthew* (Grand Rapids: Baker Book House, 1965), p. 421.

III. Covenantal Ethics

5

THE TERMS OF SOVEREIGNTY

"Make disciples of all the nations. . . , teaching them to observe all that I commanded you" (Matthew 28:19a, 20a).

The third feature of the covenant to which we now turn is *ethics*. In the ethics section of a covenant is set forth the *pattern of life*, the standards for conduct, expected under the Sovereign Covenant Maker. It is vitally important to realize that the "principle is that law is at the heart of God's covenant. The primary idea is that God wants His people to see an *ethical* relationship between cause and effect: be faithful and prosper."[1] This is true of the Great Commission in that it is a covenantal transaction. Christ acts as the Great Prophet[2] by authoritatively declaring the will of God.

Discipleship in Life

In the Great Commission proper we find in the original Greek three participles: "going," "baptizing," and "teaching." The main verbal command, which draws these three participles into its orbit, is the directive to "disciple": "Go therefore and *make disciples* of all the nations." What does it mean to "make disciples"? And how does this involve ethics? In light of some

---

1. Ray R. Sutton, *That You May Prosper: Dominion By Covenant* (Tyler, TX: Institute for Christian Economics, 1987), p. 17.
2. Deut. 18:18; John 6:14; cp. Matt. 13:57; 21:11; Luke 24:19; John 1:25, 45; Acts 3:20-25.

confusion on the whole matter, these are important and relevant questions.

Some evangelicals inadvertently water down the exhortation here. For instance, Charles Lee Feinberg writes that "Nothing could be plainer in the New Testament than that in this age of grace God uses the church, members of the body of Christ, to be witnesses throughout the earth (Mt 28:18-20; Ac 1:8)."[3]

In a book written by Wayne House and Thomas Ice, there appears an interesting statement in this regard. In the paragraph immediately following a reference to the Matthew 28 Great Commission, we find the following: "First is the word 'disciples' (Matthew 28:19)." Then a few sentences later they write: "The Greek word *mathetes* [disciple] simply means 'learner' or 'pupil,' and is one of the general terms used to describe a believer in Christ . . . . A disciple is anyone who is a believer, who is learning God's Word and is growing."[4]

What are we to make of such statements? Are they accurate summations of the Great Commission command to disciple? As a matter of fact, the statements cited are flawed and deficient on the very surface. And as such are illustrative of a widespread misapprehension of this most noble task committed to the Church.

Feinberg erroneously cites Matthew 28:18-20 as an example of which "nothing could be plainer" that Christians are "to be *witnesses* throughout the earth." As we shall see, "nothing could be plainer" than that Feinberg *misinterprets* Christ's command to Christians to "make disciples" by stating they should merely be "witnesses."

House and Ice fare little better. Although their own context is clear that they are dealing with Matthew 28:19, they speak as if the command used the *noun* "disciple" rather than the *verb* "make disciples." They end with a non-descript understanding of a "disciple": He is anyone who is a "believer" who is "grow-

---

3. Charles Lee Feinberg, "The Jew After the Rapture" in Feinberg, ed., *Prophecy and the Seventies* (Chicago: Moody Press, 1971), p. 182.
4. H. Wayne House and Thomas D. Ice, *Dominion Theology: Blessing or Curse?* (Portland, OR: Multnomah, 1988), p. 153.

ing." Growing in what? The understanding of regeneration? As a matter of fact, this deficient understanding is actually set forth as the implication by some. Megachurch fundamentalist pastor Jack Hyles[5] has written of the Great Commission: "Notice the four basic verbs: (1) *Go*. (2) *Preach*. (3) *Baptize*. (4) *Teach* them again. You teach them something after you get them saved and baptized. What do you teach them? To . . . 'observe all things whatsoever I have commanded you.' . . . Now what did He command us to do? Go, preach, baptize, then teach what He commanded us to do. So, we teach them to go, preach, and baptize, that they may teach their converts to go and preach and baptize."[6]

Or is the discipling work of the Great Commission much more than just helping people "grow"? Would not the understanding of the implications of the new life of salvation entail training in the application of God's Word to *all* of life, in that Christ's claimed authority is "in heaven and on earth" and is directed to "all the nations"?

The mission of the Church is much more than to be a witness, although certainly the Church is to be at least that (Acts 1:8). As Boettner notes: "The disciples were commanded not merely to preach, but *to make disciples of all the nations*."[7] Had the Great Commission set forth the mission solely to "preach," the Lord would have used the Greek verb *kerusso* (as in Mark 16:15). Had He meant only that His people should be a "witness," He would have used the noun *maturia* (as in Acts 1:8). But He does neither in Matthew 28:19. And the fact that He does not is terribly significant.

D. A. Carson rightly notes that *"matheteuo* ('I disciple') entails both preaching and response."[8] The proclamation of truth is

---

5. Hyles pastors the largest church in America, according to Lyle E. Schaller, "Megachurch!," *Christianity Today*, March 5, 1990, p. 22. Although there is some question as to the accuracy of the attendance figures cited by Hyles. See: Letter to the editor, from Vernon J. Norman, *Christianity Today*, May 14, 1990, p. 10.

6. Jack Hyles, *Let's Go Soul Winning* (Murfreesboro, TN: Sword of the Lord, 1962), p. 22. John R. Rice agrees in his *Why Our Churches Do Not Win Souls* (Murfreesboro: Sword of the Lord, 1966), p. 22.

7. Loraine Boettner, *The Millennium* (Nutley, NJ: Presbyterian and Reformed, 1957), p. 15.

8. D. A. Carson, "Matthew," in Frank E. Gaebelein, *The Expositor's Bible Commentary*

necessarily there, of course. But the idea of discipling involves *the proclamation of truth with a view to its effecting the appropriate response in the disciple*. In fact, "To disciple a person to Christ is to bring him into the relation of pupil to teacher [sovereignty], 'taking his yoke' of authoritative instruction (11:29) [hierarchy], accepting what he says as true because he says it and submitting to his requirements as right [ethics] because he makes them."[9]

Discipling involves turning people from sinful rebellion against God to a faithful commitment to Christ[10] and training them in the exercise of that faith commitment in all of life,[11] not just a non-descript "growing."

William Hendriksen insightfully observes: "The term 'make disciples' places somewhat more stress on the fact that the mind, as well as the heart and will, must be won for God."[12] In other words, it is designed to win the *obedience in all of life* of the disciple. It is to promote ethical covenant living. But how shall the Church win the heart to God? How may the will of man be turned to follow after His will? And since the *ministry* of the Church is to promote the worship of God in all of life, where shall God's will for all life be found? In mystic contemplation? Charismatic prophecy? Human logic? Warm feelings? Pragmatic considerations?

For the orthodox Christian, the answer should be obvious: We determine the will of God through Spirit-blessed study of the written Word of God, the Bible.[13] As the Lord says: "Go therefore and make disciples of all the nations, . . . *teaching them to observe all that I commanded you*" (Matt. 28:18-19).

(Grand Rapids: Regency Reference Library, 1984), 8:597.

9. John A. Broadus, *Commentary on the Gospel of Matthew* in Alvah Hovey, ed., *An American Commentary* (Valley Forge: Judson Press, 1886 [rep.], p. 593. Bracketed words are mine, KLG.

10. Acts 20:21; 26:18.

11. Acts 20:27; Col. 3:17; 2 Cor. 10:31; Heb. 5:11-14.

12. William Hendriksen, *Matthew (New Testament Commentary)* (Grand Rapids: Baker, 1973), p. 999.

13. Matt. 4:4; John 17:17; Acts 17:11; 2 Tim. 3:15-17; 1 Pet. 2:2; Heb. 4:12. See: John Murray, "The Guidance of the Holy Spirit" in *Collected Writings of John Murray*, vol. 1: *The Claims of Truth* (Edinburgh: Banner of Truth, 1976), pp. 186-189. Garry Friesen, *Decision Making & the Will of God: A Biblical Alternative to the Traditional View* (Portland, OR: Multnomah, 1980).

Instruction in the Word

The Christian faith is a "religion of the book." The whole Bible is, in effect, a covenant document. The orthodox Christian holds that the Bible is "inspired by God and profitable for teaching, for reproof, for correction, for training in righteousness; that the man of God may be adequate, equipped for every good work" (2 Tim. 3:16-17). He is confident that "no prophecy was ever made by an act of human will, but men moved by the Holy Spirit spoke from God" (2 Pet. 1:21). Thus, he rests assured in the "thus saith the Lord" of Scripture, because the prophets and apostles "speak not in words taught by human wisdom, but in those taught by the Spirit" (1 Cor. 2:13a).

The Christian accepts the apostolic word "not as the word of men, but for what it really is, the word of God, which also performs its work in you who believe" (1 Thess. 2:13). Therefore, he stands with Christ and Moses in the affirmation that "man shall not live on bread alone, but on every word that proceeds out of the mouth of God" (Matt. 4:4; cp. Deut. 8:3), for God's words are "words of life."[14] Consequently, the orthodox Christian holds to the absolute authority, infallibility, and inerrancy of Scripture. He believes the Great Commission invokes "all authority in heaven and earth," which entails "unlimited authority in every area" of life.[15]

God's Word is of foundational importance to the God-fearing Christian. His *spoken* Word not only brought into being all of reality,[16] but powerfully upholds the universe[17] and accomplishes His will in history.[18] The significance of God's Word is such that His Son, Jesus Christ the Lord, is called "the Word,"[19] in that He reveals the invisible God to man.[20] His *written* Word possesses the same authority for life as His spoken

---

14. John 6:68; Acts 5:20; Phil. 2:16.
15. Cleon Rogers, "The Great Commission," *Bibliotheca Sacra* 130-519 (July-Sept, 1973), 265.
16. Gen. 1; Psa. 33:6; 2 Cor. 4:6; Heb. 11:1.
17. Isa. 40:26-28; Heb. 1:3; Neh. 9:6; Acts 17:28; 2 Pet. 3:5,7.
18. Isa. 55:11; Eph. 1:11; Rev. 19:15,21.
19. John 1:1, 14; 1 John 1:1; Rev. 19:13.
20. Matt. 11:27; Luke 10:22; John 1:18; 6:46; 14:9; 17:6; 1 Jn. 5:20.

Word exercised creative power in the universe.

Here in the Great Commission the Word of God is promoted, when Christ instructs His followers: "teach them to observe all that I commanded you." But what all does this cover? Certainly it covers at least all things that He expressly taught — and thus involves much more than just "going, preaching, baptizing," as Jack Hyles, John R. Rice, and others teach. This should be apparent even on the surface, for He urges them to teach "all things (Gk: *panta*) whatever I commanded you." Since He is God,[21] His voice is the voice of authority.[22] Hence, all of His words that are recorded for us in Scripture come with commanding authority.[23]

It has been commented that "the fact that Jesus had given commands (*enteilamen*) indctes [*sic*] His authority to issue binding and lasting regulations . . . ."[24] These regulations "bind" and "regulate" the Christian's conduct in all of God's world. In fact, the command is that we "teach them to observe all that I commanded you." Thus, here "Jesus binds us to all that he has bidden us and not merely to some one or two features,"[25] as is too often the position of many Christians. Too many Christians delimit the command just to the specifically evangelistic enterprise or some other individualistic or personal aspect of Christian duty.

The Source of Instruction

This obligation to teach "all things commanded" extends even beyond His express words. *First*, despite some who would limit the scope of this command,[26] it should be observed that

---

21. John 1:1; 14:9; 20:28.

22. Matt. 7:29; Mark 1:22, 27; Luke 4:36, 32.

23. It should be noted that not *all* of Christ's words are recorded in Scripture, John 21:25. For a discussion of the question of their potential discovery and inclusion in the canon, see: Kenneth L. Gentry, Jr., *The Charismatic Gift of Prophecy: A Reformed Response to Wayne Grudem* (2nd. ed.: Memphis, TN: Footstool Publications, 1989), ch. 10, "The Problem of the 'Open Canon.'"

24. Rogers, "Great Commission," p. 265.

25. Lenski, *Matthew*, p. 1179.

26. D. A. Carson, "Matthew," in Frank E. Gaebelein, *The Expositor's Bible Commentary* (Grand Rapids: Regency Reference Library, 1984), 8:598: "The focus is on Jesus' com-

this command would include all teaching in Scripture that was *previous* to His earthly ministry.[27] Christ was careful in His ministry to uphold the integrity and relevance of God's Word in the Old Testament. Note that: (1) He came that He might live in terms of God's Law,[28] which man had broken.[29] (2) He taught the fundamental unity of both testaments (John 10:35), with the Old Testament forming the foundation of His teaching.[30] (3) He kept the Law in His daily life.[31] (4) He commanded His followers to keep the Law.[32] (5) Thus, He even upheld its civil validity (e.g., Matt. 15:3-6[33]). (6) He defined godly love in terms of the Law,[34] as did the apostles.[35]

It is important to keep in mind that the apostles themselves followed the Master in depending upon the ethical integrity and relevance of God's Law as confirmation for their instruction.[36] We should also note that true evangelism, by the very nature of the case, necessitates the preaching of the Law. The truly evangelistic encounter must deal with the sin question,

---

mands, not Old Testament law."

27. Greg L. Bahnsen, *By This Standard: The Authority of God's Law Today* (Tyler, TX: Institute for Christian Economics, 1985).

28. Psa. 40:7ff; Heb. 10:5.

29. Rom. 3:19; Gal. 3:13; 4:4-5; 1 John 3:4.

30. E.g., Matt. 4:10; John 8:17.

31. Matt. 3:15; 4:4ff; John 8:46.

32. Matt. 5:17-20; 19:16-26; Luke 16:17; John 14:15, 21; 15:10.

33. The case of the "woman caught in adultery" (John 8:1-11), rather than being an evidence of His urging the setting aside of the requirements of the Law, shows His concern for its meticulous keeping (as might be expected from Matt. 5:17-19). The Law commanded capital punishment for adultery (Lev. 20:10). Christ did not set aside that law here. Notice that He does not say, "Do not stone her." Rather, He required the maintenance of the legal protections necessary in capital punishment trials, when He said, "He who is without sin among you, let him be the first to throw a stone at her" (v. 7). God's Law requires that the witnesses in capital cases be innocent of that particular crime or sin (Deut. 19:15) and that the witnesses be the first to begin the punishment (Deut. 17:7). All of the "witnesses" against the woman turned away upon hearing this (John 8:9), even though they allegedly caught her "in the very act" (but where is the man?).

34. Matt. 7:12; 22:36-40.

35. Rom. 13:9-10; Gal. 5:14; Jms. 2:8.

36. 1 Tim. 5:17 (cp. Deut. 25:4); 2 Cor. 6:14 (cp. Deut. 22:10); Acts 23:1-5 (cp. Ex. 22:28; Lev. 19:15). See also Gal. 5:14; 1 Cor. 7:19; 14:34; 1 John 2:3; 5:3.

and sin is defined in terms of God's Law.[37] In fact, on Judgment Day men will be judged in terms of the Law's just demands.[38]

Second, His command included the yet future teaching of the apostles. Before He left this world He left the promise that He would direct the revelation that would come by means of the Holy Spirit.[39] Christ is the One who grants the Spirit.[40] His apostles were given His Spirit to lead them in the production of Scripture.[41]

In light of this, it would appear that in urging the teaching of "all things He commanded" the Great Commission urges us to promote "the whole counsel of God" (Acts 20:27). And the whole counsel of God is found in the teaching of Moses and the Prophets (the Old Testament record), in the teaching of Christ (the Gospel record), and in the teaching of His apostles (the remaining New Testament record).[42]

The Scope of Instruction

The absolutely authoritative Word of God/Christ is the believer's *blueprint* for living all of life in God's world. Consequently, true discipleship and worship, as commanded in Christ's Great Commission, will involve promoting a holistic Christian world-and-life view.[43] Christ's Commission, then, involves a

---

37. Rom. 3:20; 7:7, 13; Jms. 2:9-11; 1 John 3:4.
38. Matt. 7:23; 13:41; Luke 13:27; Rom. 2:12-15; 3:19.
39. John 14:15-18, 26; 15:26-27; 16:5-15.
40. Luke 24:49; Acts 2:32-33; Eph. 4:8.
41. Cf. 1 Cor. 2:13; 1 Thess. 1:5.
42. It is not found in any alleged charismatic prophetic utterances today. The Church is built upon an established foundation of final truth brought by the authoritative apostles and prophets, with Jesus Christ being the chief cornerstone (Eph. 2:20-21). Christ led His disciples into "all truth" (John 16:13). The completed Scripture, then, is all that is needed to "thoroughly equip" the believer for "every good work" (2 Tim. 3:16-17). The faith has been "once for all delivered to the saints" (Jude 3). See: Kenneth L. Gentry, Jr., *The Charismatic Gift of Prophecy: A Reformed Response to Wayne Grudem* (2ed.: Memphis, TN: Footstool, 1989).
43. For an illustrative sampling of the application of Scripture to various academic disciplines, see: Kenneth L. Gentry, Jr. "The Greatness of the Great Commission" in *Journal of Christian Reconstruction*, VII:2 (Winter, 1981), 42-45; Gary North, ed., *Foundations of Christian Scholarship: Essays in the Van Til Perspective* (Vallecito, CA: Ross House, 1976); and the groundbreaking, 10-volume *Biblical Blueprint Series*, edited by Gary North

radical commitment to and promotion of all Scripture as "profitable . . . that the man of God might be thoroughly furnished for every good work."[44]

Paul, as Christianity's greatest missionary, provides for us an important example in the application of this aspect of the Great Commission, when he writes: "For though we walk in the flesh, we do not war according to the flesh, for the weapons of our warfare are not of the flesh, but divinely powerful for the destruction of fortresses. We are destroying speculations and *every* lofty thing raised up against the knowledge of God, and we are taking *every* thought captive to the obedience of Christ" (2 Cor. 10:4-5, emphasis added).

Rather than conforming to the world, Paul urges a radical transforming of the mind by the ascertaining of the will of God (Rom. 12:1,2). He promoted an "exposing of the works of darkness" (Eph. 5:11), wherever they were found, in every aspect of life, because God-less thinking and acting is blindness and vanity.[45] He challenged the very intellectual underpinnings of non-Christian culture, urging their being "destroyed" (not by the sword, but by the spiritual instruments available in God's Word) and being replaced with "captive obedience" to Christ. He firmly believed that in Christ alone was "the truth"[46] and true knowledge and wisdom.[47]

Christ taught that His converts were to follow Him (John 10:27) on a new path (Matt. 7:13-14). He claimed to be "the way, the truth, and the life" (John 14:6). Thus, early Christians were initially called a people of "the way,"[48] because they followed a new way of life. They were also known as "disciples" because they were trained in the truth and application of "the way."[49] They did not simply receive "testimony" or hear

(Ft. Worth, TX: Dominion Press, 1986-87). For essays on various aspects of the Christian worldview, see also my book, *Light for the World: Studies in Reformed Theology* (Alberta, Canada: Still Waters Revival Press, forthcoming).

44. 2 Tim. 3:16-17; cp. 2 Tim. 2:21; Heb. 13:21.
45. Rom. 1:21; Eph. 4:17; Col. 2:18.
46. John 14:6; cp. John 17:17.
47. Col. 2:3, 9; cp. Prov. 1:7; 9:10.
48. Acts 9:2; 19:9, 23; 24:14, 22.
49. Acts 1:15; 6:1, 2, 7; 9:1, 10, 19, 25, 26, 36, 38; 11:26, 29; 13:52; 14:20, 22, 28;

"preaching." They responded positively to that testimony and preaching; they were "discipled" in a new faith, a new approach to all of life.[50]

Resistance to the Commission

Surprisingly, there have been several evangelicals who have recently expressed dismay over the growth in the numbers of Christians who promote God's will among *all* the affairs of men, not just the inner spiritual life of individuals and families.[51] These writers are disturbed that some Christians seek to promote the Christian faith in the world with a view to its actually prevailing among and exercising dominion over all the affairs of men. The impression left by these writers is clearly that such thinking advocates political revolution, social upheaval, and the fostering of a Church-State. Such is clearly wrong.

The rallying cry of concerned Christians is not in the least the call for dominion through political manipulation and military conquest. The promotion of *the crown rights of King Jesus*,[52] as it may be expressed, is through the means of the Great Commission's evangelistic call to disciple the nations. Clearly the means of Christ's dominion in the world is to exercise, through His people, a spiritual influence, not an influence through carnal warfare or political upheaval.[53]

15:10; 16:1; 18:23, 27; 19:1, 9; 30; 20:1; 20:7, 30; 21:4, 16.

50. Even the Jews were learning a "new" way, because they had long forsaken the written Law of God in deference to the "sayings of the elders," e.g., Matt. 15:1ff. See Gary North, *The Judeo-Christian Tradition* (Tyler, TX: Institute for Christian Economics, 1989), chaps. 6, 7, for an analysis of the anti-biblical nature of the Jewish Talmud.

51. David Wilkerson, *Set The Trumpet to Thy Mouth* (Lindale, TX: World Challenge, 1985); Jimmy Swaggert, "The Coming Kingdom," *The Evangelist* (September, 1986), pp. 4-12; House and Ice, *Dominion Theology*; Hal Lindsey, *The Road to Holocaust* (New York: Bantam, 1989).

52. Acts 17:7; Rev. 1:5-6.

53. "The basis for building a Christian society is evangelism and missions that lead to a widespread Christian revival, so that the great mass of earth's inhabitants will place themselves under Christ's protection, and then voluntarily use His covenantal laws for self-government. Christian reconstruction begins with personal conversion to Christ and self-government under God's law; then it spreads to others through revival; and only later does it bring comprehensive changes in civil law, when the vast majority of voters voluntarily agree to live under biblical blueprints." Gary North, *Political Polytheism: The Myth of Pluralism* (Tyler, TX: Institute for Christian Economics, 1989), pp. 585-586.

In fact, we are reminded once again that "The term 'make disciples' places somewhat more stress on the fact that the mind, as well as the heart and will, must be won for God."[54] The reason being that Christ's kingdom is "not of this world," that is, it does not receive its power or exercise its influence like earthly kingdoms (John 18:36). This is because it operates from "within," rather than from without.[55] Christ's authority, we must remember, is "in *heaven* and on earth"; it comes *from above* and *works within.*

The command to teach is a command to "teach them to *observe* all that I commanded you" (Matt. 28:20a). We are to urge the promotion of Christian theory *and* practice. The theoretical foundation in the Great Commission ("all authority"), gives rise to the practical duties ("go," "disciple," "baptize," "teach to observe"). In fact, it is important to note the general order of instruction in the New Testament epistles. There is the common tendency to lay down doctrinal foundations (theory) first, and then to erect upon those sure foundations ethical directives (practice).[56] That is, there is the call to "practice what you preach."[57]

Again we are reminded that conversion to the Christian faith involves the taking up of a new life style.[58] As we noted earlier, Christ claims to be "the way" of life (John 14:6). He obligates us to "follow" Him.[59] He promises us blessings for building our lives on Him and His teaching, and warns us that a refusal to build our entire lives on Him and His doctrine will eventuate in collapse and ruin.[60] Thus, the implementation of

---

54. William Hendriksen, *Matthew* (*New Testament Commentary*) (Grand Rapids: Baker, 1973), p. 999.

55. Matt. 13:33; Luke 17:21; 1 Cor. 4:20; 2 Cor. 10:4-5.

56. Although this is no hard-and-fast rule with water-tight compartments, the general tendency is especially evident in Paul's writings. Paul urges a specific conduct based on particular doctrinal considerations, often by the use of a "therefore" (Rom. 1-11, cp. 12:1ff; Eph. 1-3, cp. 5:1ff; Phil. 1-3, cp. 4:1ff; Col. 1-2, cp. 3:1ff)

57. See: Matt. 7:24; 21:28-32; 23:3; Jms. 2:22.

58. Luke 3:8; Rom. 6:18; 1 Cor. 6:10-11; Eph. 2:2-3; 4:17, 22, 28; 5:8; Col. 3:5-8; 1 Thess. 1:9.

59. Matt. 10:38; 16:24; John 8:12; 10:27; 12:26.

60. Matt. 7:24-27; Luke 11:28; John 13:17; 14:15, 23, 24; John 15:14.

His truth claims in every endeavor and walk of life is here rightly commanded of us.

Those who neglect the social and cultural ramifications of Christ's Word relegate Scripture to practical irrelevance regarding the larger issues of life. Like the Old Testament, the New Testament promotes a Christian view of social duty and involvement. Of course, it is concerned with marriage and divorce (Matt. 5:27-32; Luke 16:18; 1 Cor. 7:1-10), family relations (Eph. 5:22-33; Col. 3:18-20), and child rearing (Eph. 6:1-4; Col. 3:21), as all agree. But it also instructs us regarding the rich man's duty to the poor (Matt. 25:31-46; Luke 16:19-25; 2 Cor. 8:13ff), employer-employee relationships (Eph. 6:5-9; Luke 17:10), honest wages (1 Tim. 5:18; Luke 10:7), free-market bargaining (Matt. 20:1-15), private property rights (Acts 5:4), godly citizenship and the proper function of the state (Rom. 13:1-7; 1 Pet. 2:13-17), the family as the primary agency of welfare (1 Tim. 5:8), proper use of finances (Matt. 25:14ff), the dangers of debt (Rom. 13:8), the morality of investment (Matt. 25:14-30), the obligation to leaving an inheritance (2 Cor. 12:14), penal restraints upon criminals (Rom. 13:4; 1 Tim. 1:8-10), lawsuits (1 Cor. 6:1-8), and more. In doing so, it reflects and supplements the socio-cultural concern of the Old Testament, urging the people of God to live *all of life* under Christ's authority, not just the inner-personal or family or church areas of life. Hence, the command to "observe all things I commanded you."

Yet there are those in evangelical circles who would attempt to dissuade in-depth social involvement for the believer. One missions textbook does so:

Christ is the wisest of all philosophers. He is the wisdom of God, yet founded no philosophical school. Christ is the greatest of all scholars and educators, yet He instituted no educational system. Christ is the greatest benefactor and philanthropist, yet He founded no social welfare societies, institutions of philanthropic foundations. Christ was "Christian presence" with deepest concerns for freedom, social uplift, equality, moral reformation and economic justice. Yet Christ founded no organization or institutions to initiate, propagate or implement the ideals which He incarnated . . . Christ did not become involved in processions against Roman overlords, slavery, social and economic injustices, or marches for civil rights, higher wages, or better education.[61]

That book continues elsewhere:

> We are sent not to preach sociology but salvation; not economics but evangelism; not reform but redemption; not culture but conversion; not a new social order but a new birth; not revolution but regeneration; not renovation but revival; not resuscitation but resurrection; not a new organization but a new creation; not democracy but the gospel; not civilization but Christ; we are ambassadors not diplomats.[62]

But should we not preach "biblical sociology" so that the recipients of salvation might know how they ought to behave as social creatures? Should we not preach "biblical economics" to those who are evangelized, so that men might know how to be good stewards of the resources God has entrusted into their care, resources they use every day of their lives? Should we not promote a "biblical culture" to those who are converted so that they might labor toward a transforming of a godless culture into a God-honoring one? On and on we could go in response.

There are even Christian colleges advertising along these lines. The following advertisement was see in *Faith For the Family*, advertising a Christian university: "Christianize the world? FORGET IT! . . . . Try to bring Christian values, morals, precepts, and standards upon a lost world and you're wasting your time . . . . Evangelize — preach the Gospel; snatch men as brands from the burning . . . . All your preaching won't change the world, but the Gospel 'is the power of God unto salvation to everyone that believeth.'"[63] (We might ask: What academic course work could be assigned that would be consistent with such a view of Christian thought? What textbooks does such a

---

61. George W. Peters, *A Biblical Theology of Missions* (Chicago: Moody Press, 1972), p. 211.
62. *Ibid.*, p. 209.
63. Cited in Herbert W. Bowsher, "Will Christ Return 'At Any Moment'?" in *The Journal of Christian Reconstruction* 7:2 (Winter, 1981) 48.

university assign? The answer is obvious: textbooks written either by humanists or by Christians who do not share this university's presuppositions. By the way, just for the record, until the "name inflation" of the 1970s, a university was an academic institution that granted the Ph.D degree – G.N.)

Another evangelical writer agrees, when he comments on the Great Commission: "What we are to *obey* is modeled for us in the examples of the life of Christ and the Apostles. They did not call for political revolution, organize a political party, or plot the systematic takeover of society. Instead they spent their energy saving souls and transforming the lives of those converts into citizens of God's spiritual kingdom."[64] Unfortunately, the way the statement is framed ("revolution," "political party," "takeover") puts the worst possible light on the spiritual call to socio-cultural involvement. Our weapons are not carnal for political revolution, but spiritual (2 Cor. 10:4-5). Our effectiveness is not through political parties, but through the Church (Eph. 1:19-21), prayer (1 Tim. 2:2-5; 1 Pet. 3:12), and godly labor (Luke 19:13; 1 Pet. 2:15-16). Our goal is not to "takeover" as in a coup, but to win through powerful word (Heb. 4:12; Eph. 6:17). As one writer has put it: "the labor is ours; the subduing is His."[65]

Conclusion

The Great Commission, then, urges us to live *all* of life for the glory of Christ, to *observe all things* whatsoever Christ commands us in His Word. We are to do *all* things to God's glory,[66] because all men and things have been created for His glory and are expected to bring Him glory.[67] We are to love God with "all our heart, all our mind, all our soul, and all our strength,"[68] for He has redeemed us in order to purify us from "all lawlessness" (Tit. 2:14, Gk.) so that we might be "zeal-

---

64. Lindsey, *Road to Holocaust*, p. 279.
65. Herschell H. Hobbs, *An Exposition of the Gospel of Matthew* (Grand Rapids: Baker, 1965), p. 422
66. Rom. 14:7-9; 1 Cor. 10:31; Col. 3:17; 1 Pet. 4:11.
67. Eccl. 12:13; Acts 17:26-31; Col. 1:16; Rev. 4:11.
68. Matt. 22:37; Mark 12:30, 33; Luke 10:27.

ous of good works" in all of life.[69] The winning of the mind and will of the lost will involve teaching all things Christ teaches us in His Word, in both Old and New Testaments.

69. Tit. 2:14; Eph. 2:10.

6

THE COMMITMENT TO SOVEREIGNTY

"Baptizing them in the name of the Father and the Son and the Holy Spirit" (Matthew 28:19b).

The fourth feature of the covenant is the requirement of an oath, often taken in conjunction with some ceremonial action. In this oath-taking ceremony, the covenant is publicly set forth as a solemn obligation under the covenantal sovereign and the historical administration of his authority. It obliges the covenant recipient to live according to the sovereign's stipulations. Divine covenants, because of the very nature of the Sovereign, involve worship. In the Great Commission, we discover both worship and the ordaining of the oath-ceremony.

All that has been established heretofore regarding the obligation to subdue all of culture for Christ must *never* be severed from its spiritual foundations in the adoration and worship of God. We must always press the spirituality principle of the kingdom work of the Church by noting its redemptive starting point and worship emphasis. As Geerhardus Vos puts it:

Jesus' doctrine of the kingdom as both inward and outward, coming first in the heart of man and afterwards in the external world, upholds *the primacy of the spiritual and ethical* over the physical. The invisible world of the inner religious life, the righteousness of the disposition, the sonship of God are in it made supreme, the essence of the kingdom, the ultimate realities to which everything else is subordinate.[1]

The Great Commission is *not* just a tool of cultural transformation, nor is it *initially* such. The cultural effects of the Great Commission flow from the redemptive power that is inherent in Christ's kingdom.

In the oath-worship aspect of the Commission, we have Christ exhibited in His priestly office. He is our Great High Priest, Who secures our redemption, which is symbolized and sealed to us in baptism.

Baptism and Worship

In the very context of the giving of the Great Commission we see the response of the delighted disciples to the presence of the risen Christ: "And when they saw Him, they worshiped Him" (Matt. 28:17a). Upon this notice, the Great Commission is given (Matt. 28:18-20). The going and the discipling of the Great Commission are a going for and a discipling under the authority of One who is infinitely worthy of our worship.[2] These "disciples" saw Christ and "worshiped Him." As these disciples were immediately instructed to "disciple all nations," they obviously were to instruct all nations in the worship of Christ.

Without a doubt the starting point of Christ's gracious influence among men is the personal salvation wrought by the sovereign grace of almighty God.[3] Evangelicals agree on this point, and I certainly confirm this truth in this book. Because of the inherent depravity of man,[4] man cannot know the things of God.[5] Nor can he save himself or even prepare himself for

---

1. Geerhardus Vos, *The Teaching of Jesus Concerning the Kingdom of God and the Church* (Nutley, NJ: Presbyterian and Reformed, rep. 1972), p. 103. (This is the title given on the title page. The title shown on the cover is only: *The Kingdom of God and the Church*.)
2. Eph. 1:20-21; Phil. 2:9-11; Heb. 1:6; Rev. 5:9-14; 5:3-4.
3. His influence is as a king over a spiritual kingdom, Matt. 4:23; John 3:3; Acts 8:12; Col. 1:13.
4. Psa. 51:5; Jer. 17:9; Rom. 3:10; Eph. 2:3.
5. John 3:19; 1 Cor. 2:14; Eph. 4:17-19.

salvation.[6] In addition, neither can he function properly in God's world.[7] This is where the Great Commission comes in: it harnesses the power of God to effect a radical change in the heart and mind of man. Based on the plan of God, founded upon the work of Christ, effected by the operation of the Holy Spirit, the gospel brings eternal salvation to sinners otherwise hopelessly lost. And this points to the importance of baptism for the Commission.

Christ ordained baptism as a sign[8] and seal[9] of His gracious covenant. Baptism primarily and fundamentally signifies union with Christ, a union that entails faith in Christ, and cleansing from sin.[10] The very formula of baptism given in the Great Commission itself points to the truth of union with Christ (with the fuller notion of that union involving the Triune God): "baptizing them in the name of the Father and the Son and the Holy Spirit" (Matt. 28:19b).[11]

But the promotion of personal, individual, spiritual salvation, wherein the convert is cleansed from his sin and united with Christ, is not the end-all of the Great Commission. Here we rephrase the Gaines Dobbins interchange mentioned earlier. To the question: "Is not conversion the end of the Great Commission?" we reply, "Yes, but which end?"

---

6. Job 14:4; Jer. 13:23; John 6:44, 65; Rom. 3:10; 8:8.

7. Matt. 12:33; Acts 26:18-20; Rom. 8:7,8; Eph. 2:1,2.

8. As a "sign" baptism is an external action visible to the senses that portrays the internal grace of Holy Spirit baptism, which spiritually effects union with Christ. Notice the close connection of water and Spirit baptism in Scripture, Matt. 3:11; Mark 1:8; Luke 3:16; John 1:33; Acts 1:5; 2:38; 10:47; 11:16; 19:1-6; 1 Cor. 12:13.

9. As a "seal" of the covenant, baptism is the divinely ordained confirmation and guarantee of the spiritual transaction effected. Note that (1) Baptism is specifically said to have taken over for circumcision in the New Testament era (Col. 2:11-12), and circumcision is called a "seal" by Paul (Rom. 4:11). The sealing action is effected by the Holy Spirit (1 Cor. 1:21-22; Eph. 1:13ff; 4:30). (2) This is why baptism can be so closely associated with the spiritual effects that it virtually appears to stand for those effects (Acts 2:38; 22:16; Rom. 6:3; Gal. 3:27; Col. 2:12; 1 Pet. 3:21). It is the seal of those actual spiritual effects.

10. See discussion below, pp. 84-90.

11. See the trinitarian involvement in the believer's union in John 14:16, 17, 23; 17:21-23.

Baptism and Authority

Spiritual union with Christ is signified in ceremonial baptism. And this union is essential to the ultimate Christian cultural renewal resultant from the effects of great numbers of conversions.[12] And the formula of baptism emphasizes that union in an important manner. Christ commands His Church to baptize converts *"in* the *name* of the Father and the Son and the Holy Spirit" (Matt. 28:19b). Now what is the significance of baptizing "in" the "name" of the Triune God?

The Greek preposition *eis* ("in") is here used in such a way as to express "the notion of sphere."[13] That is, this baptism is a sign and seal of the newly-won disciple's being "in the sphere of " or "coming-under-the-Lordship-of " the Father, Son, and Holy Spirit.[14] Or, as its result is related elsewhere, the convert is "in Christ."[15] At the moment of salvation, then, the redeemed sinner is removed from the realm of Satan and his dominion-rule[16] to the realm of the Triune God and his dominion-rule (Acts 26:18).[17] Interestingly, in the Book of Acts, where we have the historical record of the early Church's missionary labor, Christ is called "Lord" at least twenty-six times, and probably as many as ninety-two times.[18] He is called "Sav-

---

12. See Chapter 4 for the promise of the massive, worldwide redemptive effects of the Great Commission.

13. See: A. T. Robertson, *A Greek Grammar in the Light of Historical Research* (Nashville: Broadman, 1934), p. 592; R. C. H. Lenski, *The Interpretation of St. Matthew's Gospel* (Columbus, OH: Wartburg, 1943), p. 1175.

14. D. A. Carson, "Matthew" in Frank E. Gaebelein, *The Expositor's Bible Commentary* (Grand Rapids: Regency Reference Library, 1984), 8:597.

15. See the following Pauline references to being "in Christ": Rom. 8:2; 12:5; 16:3; 16:10; 1 Cor. 1:2, 30; 3:1 4:15, 17; 15:22; 16:24; 2 Cor. 1:21; 2:14; 5:17; 12:2; Gal. 1:22; 2:4; 3:28; 5:6; 6:15; Eph.1:1; 1:3; 2:6; 2:10; 2:13; 3:6; Phil. 1:1; 2:1; 2:5; 3:3; 4:21; Col. 1:2, 4, 28; 1 Thess. 2:14; 4:16; 1 Tim. 1:14; 2 Tim. 1:1, 9; 2:1; 3:12; Phile. 1:8, 23.

16. Greg L. Bahnsen, "The Person, Work, and Present Status of Satan," *The Journal of Christian Reconstruction* I (Winter, 1974):11-43.

17. See note 23 below. For a study of there being a new master over the believer, see Romans 6. Consult John Murray, *The Epistle to the Romans* (*New International Commentary on the New Testament*) (Grand Rapids: Wm. B. Eerdmans, 1959), vol. 1, ch. 6.

18. The following are the indisputable references to Jesus as "Lord" in Acts. See: Acts 1:21; 2:36; 4:33; 7:59; 8:16; 9:5, 17, 27, 29; 10:36; 11:17, 20; 15:11, 26; 16:31; 19:5, 10, 13, 17; 20:21, 24, 35; 21:13; 22:8; 26:15; 28:31. Many other references to the "Lord" (unqualified by the addition of "Jesus" or .''Christ") undoubtedly refer to Him as well,

ior" but twice.[19] *The Scripture clearly emphasizes His lordship in salvation and life.* And, of course, the whole conception of discipleship, as conceived in the Great Commission, implies a master/student relationship between the Lord and the convert.

The authority of the Triune God is also involved in baptism by the expression indicating the disciple is baptized in His "name." It is true that ancient Jews often used "the name" as a substitute for saying the holy name of Jehovah (in fear of accidentally breaching the Third Commandment). Nevertheless, such is not the case in Matthew 28:19. Rather, "the name," coupled with the baptismal action here, indicates "ownership."[20] It is not merely a Hebraism or a circumlocution for the person of God.[21]

There is good evidence that the terminology employed here was used both inside and outside of Christian circles in a way helpful to the understanding of its usage in Matthew 28. Greek scholars have found that "the use of name (*onoma*) here is a common one in the Septuagint and the papyri for power or authority."[22] For instance, Pagan soldiers swore *into the name* or possession of the god Zeus upon their entry into military service. And in financial matters money was paid *into the name* or account or possession of someone. "Accordingly in the present passage the baptized may be said to be translated into the possession of the Father, Jesus Christ, and His Spirit."[23]

All of this is most significant. At conversion to the Lord Jesus Christ, men bow to a new Lord and Master, and receive the sign and seal of His kingdom. Consequently, in this baptismal

---

possibly adding to these another sixty-six samples.

19. Acts 5:31; 13:23.
20. R. E. Nixon, *Matthew* in D. B. Guthrie and J. A. Motyer, eds., *The Eerdmans Bible Commentary* (3rd. ed.: Grand Rapids: Wm. B. Eerdmans, 1970), p. 850.
21. Robertson, *Grammar*, p. 649.
22. A. T. Robertson, *Word Pictures in the New Testament* (Nashville: Broadman, 1930), 1:245.
23. F. W. Green, *The Gospel According to Saint Matthew* in Thomas Strong and Herbert Wild, eds., *The Clarendon Bible* (Oxford: Clarendon, 1960), p. 258. Other references bringing the Trinity together in specific contexts include: Matt. 3:13-17; 1 Cor. 12:4-6; 2 Cor. 1:21-22; 13:14; Gal. 4:6; Eph. 1:3-6; 4:4-6; 2 Thess. 2:13-14; 1 Pet. 1:2; Rev. 1:4-6. See also: *The Didache* 7:1-13 and Justin Martyr, *First Apology* 61.

act of worship, there is a public, sacramental declaration of the exchange from one realm of authority (Satan's) to another (God's).[24] This supplements the idea of Christian cultural renewal, for the baptizand is now obligated to live all of life in terms of the covenantal obligations of the new Master as opposed to the old.

Baptism and Oath

Throughout this book, I have been demonstrating that *the Great Commission is a covenant obligation*. Consequently, it requires a covenant oath of commitment to the terms of the covenant. Baptism is the sign and seal of the covenant and involves a covenant oath. As I discussed in Chapter 2, the oath section of the covenant involves sanctions. The covenant holds forth the prospect of blessings for obedience to the terms of the covenant and threatens curses for disobedience. Although we are prone only to think of the glorious promises associated with baptism, there are *negative sanctions* involved in baptism, as well.

As a sign and seal of our redemption, baptism speaks of our salvation and the newness of life, which salvation brings. Just as the old creation (the physical world) emerged from under the waters (Gen. 1:1-10), so does the new creation (the redeemed world, i.e. salvation). In the pouring out of the waters of baptism upon the convert,[25] we receive the sign of the coming of the Holy Spirit, Who effects our union with the Triune God, cleansing from sin, and faith in Christ. Baptism, then, speaks of blessing and forgiveness.

Yet, baptism also strongly exhibits judgment. The first mention of baptism in the New Testament is under John Baptist's ministry. John baptizes with a view to repentance from sin, in

---

24. Acts 26:18; Col. 1:13; 2 Tim. 2:26; Heb. 2:14-15; Eph. 2:3. See also: John 5:24; Eph. 5:8; 1 John 3:8; 4:4; 5:19.

25. In Scripture there is established a conscious, deliberate correspondence between Holy Spirit baptism and water baptism (Matt. 3:11; Mark 1:8; John 1:33; Acts 1:4,5; 10:44-48; 11:15-16). The one is the sign of the other. Consequently, they correspond in modal representation. The Holy Spirit is always said to be poured out or sprinkled down upon the object of His sanctifying operations: Prov. 1:23; Isa. 32:15; 44:3; Eze. 36:25-28; 39:29; Joel 2:28-29; Zech. 12:10; Acts 2:15-17, 33; 10:44-45; Tit. 3:5,6.

anticipation of coming judgment.[26] Later, Christ refers to His looming judgment, suffering, and death as a "baptism."[27] The writer of Hebrews also speaks of the "various baptisms"[28] in the Old Testament, "baptisms" performed with the blood of slain sacrificial animals, which clearly speak of judgmental death (Heb. 9:10, 13, 19, 21).

Christian baptism is itself tied to judgment. The Pentecostal call to baptism was given in the shadow of looming fiery judgment: the destruction of Jerusalem (Acts 2:19-21, 40-41). Likewise, Peter relates baptism to life and death issues, when he speaks of it in the context of Noah's Flood (1 Pet. 3:20-21). Thus, the escape from judgment that baptism relates is through the redemptive sufferings of Christ, as Paul makes clear in Romans 6. There he specifically mentions the death aspect entailed in baptism, when he says: "Therefore we were buried with Him through baptism into death."[29]

In the final analysis it may be said that baptism is "an oath-sign of allegiance to Christ the Lord. . . . And if the immediate function of baptism in covenant administration is to serve as the ritual of an oath of discipleship, we have in that another indication that baptism is a symbolic portrayal of the judgment of the covenant. For, as we have seen, covenant oath rituals were enactments of the sanctions invoked in the oath."[30] As Gary North puts it: ". . . *where there is an oath, there is also implicitly a curse. Without the presence of a curse, there can be no oath.*"[31]

---

26. Matt. 3:7-12; Luke 3:3-9. See: Richard Flinn, "Baptism, Redemptive History, and Eschatology" in James B. Jordan, ed., *The Failure of American Baptist Culture*, vol. 1 of *Christianity and Civilization* (Tyler, TX: Geneva Divinity School, 1982), p. 119, n. 26.

27. Matt. 20:22-23; Mark 10:38-39; Luke 12:50.

28. The Greek of Hebrews 9:10 has *baptismois* as the word rendered "washings." It is the noun form of the verb *baptizo*, "to baptize."

29. Rom. 6:4; cp. Col. 2:11-12.

30. Meredith G. Kline, *By Oath Consigned: A Reinterpretation of the Covenant Signs of Circumcision and Baptism* (Grand Rapids: Wm. B. Eerdmans, 1968), p. 81. For a corrective of some imbalance in Kline, see Flinn, "Baptism, Redemptive History, and Eschatology," pp. 122-131.

31. Gary North, *The Sinai Strategy: Economics and the Ten Commandments* (Tyler, TX: Institute for Christian Economics, 1986), p. 56.

Baptism and Culture

Most Christians agree that baptism is the appropriate, biblical sign to be applied to new converts to the faith. We see a number of examples in the New Testament of individuals receiving baptism upon their conversion under the influence of the Great Commission. We think of the Ethiopian eunuch, Paul, Cornelius, Lydia, the Philippian jailer, Crispus, and Gaius.[32]

But in that the Great Commission is a covenantal commission, baptism cannot be limited to an individualistic focus. Just as the Great Commission has a corporate influence, so does baptism itself. And this corporate design entails the baptism of the *families* of believers.

In God's covenantal dealings with His people, there is what we may call the principle of *family solidarity*.[33] We see this great principle at work in various examples in Scripture. For instance, although the Bible teaches that "*Noah* found grace in the eyes of the Lord" (Gen. 6:8), his entire *family* was brought into the Ark for protection, due to God's gracious covenant.[34] Likewise, God's covenant was established with Abraham (Gen. 12:1-3) — *and with his seed* (Gen. 17:7). God's gracious covenant was designed to run in family generations,[35] just as were His fearsome covenant curses.[36]

Because of this, God graciously sanctifies (sets apart) the offspring of the covenantal faithful. Even in the New Testament God draws a distinction between the children of His people and the children of non-believers: "For the unbelieving husband is sanctified by the wife, and the unbelieving wife is sanctified by the husband: *else were your children unclean; but now are they holy*" (1 Cor. 7:14).[37] This explains why Christ lays His hands on

---

32. Acts 8:38; 9:18; 10:48; 16:15, 33; 1 Cor. 1:14.

33. See: Kenneth L. Gentry, Jr., *Infant Baptism: A Duty of God's People* (Mauldin, SC: GoodBirth Pubs., 1982).

34. Gen. 6:18; 7:1, 7.

35. Josh. 2:12-13; Psa. 37:17,18; 103:17-18; 105:8; 115:13-14; Prov. 3:33.

36. Exo. 20:5; 34:6,7; Deut. 5:9. Note: Gen. 9:24-25; Hos. 9:11-17; Psa. 109:1,2,9,10; Prov. 3:33.

37. The principle is found in Romans 14:17, as well: "For if the firstfruit be holy, the

infants of His followers, to bless them.[38] When Paul writes to the "saints" (set apart ones) in a particular locality,[39] he includes commands for the children, who are numbered among the saints.[40]

In addition, we may note that New Testament blessings, like those of the Old Testament, are framed in terms *inclusive* of family generations, rather than in terms *excluding* family generations: the promise is to believers and their children.[41] There is *nothing* in the New Testament that undermines and invalidates the Old Testament covenantal principle of family solidarity. In fact, everything confirms its continuing validity. Thus, a covenantal understanding of baptism leads inexorably to infant baptism. In order briefly to demonstrate this, let us first consider the Old Testament sign of the covenant: circumcision. Then we will show the elements of continuity between Old Testament circumcision and New Testament baptism.

Old Testament Circumcision

Clearly circumcision was *the* sign of the covenant in the Old Testament era, as is evident in the Abrahamic Covenant (Gen. 17: 7, 10-11).[42] In fact, Stephen calls it "the covenant of circumcision" (Acts 7:8). And circumcision represented *deeply spiritual* truths in Israel.

1. Circumcision represented union and communion with God. In Genesis 17:10-11 circumcision is spoken of as the sign of God's covenant with His people: "This is My covenant which you shall keep, between Me and you and your descendants after you: Every male child among you shall be circumcised; and you shall be circumcised in the flesh of your foreskins, and it shall be a sign of the covenant between Me and you." For one not to be circumcised was to be in breach of the covenant and

---

lump is also holy: and if the root be holy, so are the branches."
38. Cp. Luke 18:15-17 with Matt. 19:13-14.
39. Eph. 1:1; Col. 1:2.
40. Eph. 6:1, 4; Col. 3:20-21.
41. Acts 2:38,39; 16:31; 11:14.
42. The words "circumcision" and its negative "uncircumcision" appear seventy-one times in the Old Testament and fifty-four times in the New Testament.

would exclude the uncircumcised person from the people of God: "And the uncircumcised male child, who is not circumcised in the flesh of his foreskin, that person shall be cut off from his people; he has broken My covenant" (Gen. 17:17).

Israel was very personally and deeply in union and communion with God; she did not exist merely in a political relationship with Him.[43] In fact, the highest blessing of God's covenant with Abraham, which was sealed in circumcision, was: "I will be your God and you will be my people."[44]

2. Circumcision symbolically represented the removal of the defilement of sin. Often in the Old Testament we hear of the call to "circumcise the heart,"[45] i.e., from uncleanness. This deeply spiritual call shows the sacramental relation between the outward, physical act of circumcision and the inward, spiritual reality of cleansing from sin.

3. Circumcision sealed faith. In the New Testament, the "Apostle of Faith" clearly spoke of Old Testament circumcision's relationship to faith, the fundamental Christian virtue: Abraham "received the sign of circumcision, a seal of the righteousness of the faith which he had" (Rom. 4:11). Circumcision is a sign and seal of the righteousness that results from faith. And Abraham is the pre-eminent example of justification by faith for the apostles.[46] In fact, elsewhere Paul relates circumcision to the spiritual realities of salvation through faith.[47]

New Testament Baptism

In the New Testament phase of the covenant, baptism becomes the sign of the covenant.[48] Hence, the Great Commission's enforcement of baptism upon the converts to the faith (Matt. 28:19). Of baptism we may note that it represents the

---

43. Gen. 17:7, 11; Exo. 6:7; 29:45; Lev. 26:12.
44. Gen. 17:7; Exo. 5:2ff; 6:7; 29:45; Lev. 26:12; Deut. 7:9; 29:14-15; 2 Sam. 7:24; Jer. 24:7; 31:33; 32:38; Eze. 11:20; 34:24; 36:28; 37:23; Zech. 8:8. In addition, the phrase "My people" occurs over 200 times in the Old Testament.
45. Deut. 10:16; 30:6; Isa. 52:1; Jer. 4:4; 6:10; 9:26; Eze. 44:7-9.
46. Rom. 4:3, 9, 12, 16; Gal. 3:6-9, 14; Heb. 11:8, 17; Jms. 2:23.
47. Rom. 2:28,29; Phil. 3:3; Col. 2:11.
48. Mark 16:16; Acts 2:38; 8:12; 10:48; 22:16; 1 Pet. 3:21.

same spiritual truths as circumcision: (1) Union and communion with the Lord,[49] cleansing from the defilement of sin,[50] and faith.[51]

In fact, baptism specifically replaced circumcision, for it is written of Christians: "In Him you were also circumcised with the circumcision made without hands, by putting off the body of the sins of the flesh, *by the circumcision of Christ, buried with Him in baptism*, in which you also were raised with Him through faith in the working of God, who raised Him from the dead" (Col. 2:11-12, emphasis added). Therefore, it is not surprising that, following the pattern set by Old Testament circumcision, baptism is mentioned in conjunction with the promise to *families* (Acts 2:38,39) and that examples of whole *family* baptism are recorded.[52]

In Acts 16:14-15 we read: "Now a certain woman named Lydia heard us. . . . The Lord opened her heart to heed the things spoken by Paul. And when she and her household were baptized, she begged us, saying, 'If you have judged me to be faithful to the Lord, come to my house and stay.' And she constrained us." Notice that the Lord is said to have opened *Lydia's* heart, yet "she *and her household* were baptized." This is precisely parallel to the situation with circumcision in the Old Testament.[53]

Thus, the covenantal principle of family solidarity continues from the Old Testament into the New Testament. Infant baptism, then, is justified on the following grounds, to name but a few: (1) Circumcision and baptism represent the same spiritual truths. Circumcision was applied to infants, so why not bap-

---

49. Rom. 6:3-6; 1 Cor. 12:13; Gal. 3:27,28; Col. 2:11,12.
50. Acts 2:38; 22:16; 1 Pet. 3:21. Compare also the relation between baptism and the "baptism of fire," which is a purging and purifying fire: Matt. 3:11; Mark 1:8; Luke 3:16; Acts 1:5.
51. Mark 16:16; Acts 8:36-37; 16:14-15, 33-34.
52. Acts 16:15, 33; 1 Cor. 1:16. Interestingly, there are but twelve recorded episodes of Christian baptism in the New Testament (Acts 2:41; 8:12, 13, 38; 9:18; 10:48; 16:15, 33; 18:8; 19:5; 1 Cor. 1:14, 16). Yet, three of these are household baptisms. Significantly, there are *no* instances of Christian parents presenting their children for baptism *after* a child's conversion.
53. Gen. 17:12, 13, 23, 27.

tism? (2) Baptism is specifically said to replace circumcision, so why not for infants? (3) Redemptive promises are issued in such a way as to include believers and their seed, so why not baptize both? (4) The children of believers are said to be "clean" and "holy," so why not apply the symbol of cleansing to them? (5) Household baptisms appear in the New Testament record, in some cases even though only the parent is said to have believed. (6) There is no record of the repeal of the inclusion of children in the covenant promises.

The family represents the child's first experience with society. In that the family is the training ground for mature living in society (Deut. 6:6ff; 1 Tim. 3:4-5, 12; 5:8),[54] baptism carries with it strong cultural implications.

Conclusion

The Great Commission commands the baptizing of disciples to Jesus Christ. In the action of baptism there is the establishing of a covenantal relation between God and the disciple and his seed. That covenantal relation promises reward and blessing for faithfulness to the terms of the covenant; it threatens wrath and curse for unfaithfulness. And those covenant sanctions are applied at the smallest foundational society: the family.

Too many Christians lightly regard baptism today. But its close attachment in the Great Commission to "all authority in heaven and on earth" should lead the knowledgeable Christian to a high regard for baptism. Covenantal oaths are binding obligations — eternally binding. "To whom much is given, much is required" (Luke 12:48).

---

54. See: Gary North, *Tools of Dominion: The Case Laws of Exodus* (Tyler, TX: Institute for Christian Economics, 1990), Chapters 4-5.

7

THE CONTINUANCE OF SOVEREIGNTY

"And lo, I am with you always, even to the end of the age" (Matthew 28:20b).

As I have been noting throughout this study, the greatness of the Great Commission largely has been overlooked by modern Christians. In this chapter, I will consider another aspect of the Commission's greatness that has been diminished at the hands of too many well-meaning expositors of Scripture: The expected outcome of the Great Commission in history. By way of introduction and before actually demonstrating the reasons for the progress of the gospel, I will state briefly what I believe those prospects are to be. Then I will return to provide the biblical foundation supportive of them, as found in the Great Commission and elsewhere.

The expectation of the Commission's influence is that the gospel of Jesus Christ will gradually and increasingly triumph throughout the world until the large majority of men, with their cultures and nations, are held in its gracious and holy sway. The ultimate effect will be that unparalleled (though never perfect) righteousness, peace, and prosperity will prevail throughout the earth. In other words, the Bible holds forth a gloriously optimistic prospect for the future conversion of men and nations during this present gospel age. This view of the progress of history is known as *postmillennialism*,[1] for it teaches that Christ will return after millennial conditions are spread throughout the world.

Now to the task at hand. Regarding the bright future of a world won by the Great Commission, let us consider, first:

The Commission's Empowerment

This point must be emphasized: *No optimistic expectation for the future of mankind convincingly can be argued on a secular base.* This glorious postmillennial prospect is not in any way, shape, or form rooted in any humanistic theory or on the basis of naturalistic evolutionary forces.[2] We cannot have a high estimation of the prospects of man's future based on man in himself, for "the mind set on the flesh is hostile toward God; for it does not subject itself to the law of God, for it is not even able to do so; and those who are in the flesh cannot please God" (Rom. 8:7-8). When left to himself, man's world is corrupted and destroyed, a classic illustration being in the days of Noah (Gen. 6:5).

Neither is the hope for the progress of mankind under the gospel related to the Christian's self-generated strength, wisdom, or cleverness.[3] Left to our own efforts, we Christians too quickly learn that "apart from Me you can do nothing" (John

---

1. For a definition of "postmillennialism," see Chapter 11.

2. It is interesting to read Ecclesiastes and note the comparing of the view of life from "under the sun" (Eccl. 1:14; 2:11, 17) with a view of life from the divine perspective. The "under the sun" view parallels perfectly the secular humanistic view, that cuts itself off from the God of Scripture. All becomes "vanity and vexation of spirit" in such a worldview.

3. It seems that too many even among evangelicals see evangelism as a manipulative method, rather than a delivering of the message of truth. One of the great evangelists of the last century, Dwight L. Moody, is praised by one writer in that he: "was the creator of many innovations in evangelism, such as the effective use of publicity, organization, and advertising, and in so doing he 'completed the reduction of evangelism to a matter of technique and personality.'" George Dollar, *A History of Fundamentalism in America* (Greenville, SC: Bob Jones University, 1973), p. xi. Megachurch fundamentalist pastor Jack Hyles has even taught the necessity of having fresh breath when doing personal evangelism. This is because bad breath may turn off the potential convert, who may then die and go to hell. Jack Hyles, *Let's Go Soul Winning* (Murfreesboro, TN: Sword of the Lord, 1968).

15:5). In fact, this is well illustrated in the historical context in which the Great Commission itself was given. *The Commission was issued by Christ to a small body of fearful Christians, who had very recently forsaken Him and had fled.*[4] These men fearfully hid themselves due to the violent opposition to Christ generated by the Jews and exercised by the Roman Empire,[5] an opposition He prophesied would only get worse in their own generation.[6]

Yet now Christ comes to command these cowardly disciples to take the gospel "to all nations" (Matt. 28:19), beginning first at Jerusalem (Luke 24:47)! They were now being instructed in the engagement of preaching the name of Christ in Jerusalem, the capital of Israel and the site of Christ's crucifixion, and Rome, the capital of "the nations" of the Roman empire under whose authority the crucifixion had been performed! How can they take heart in such a fearful prospect? Surely such would put their lives on the line before vehement Jewish opposition[7] and an inconsistent Roman legal system![8] And how may we today expect to have any success with the gospel against our opposition? The humanist opposition is well funded, adequately equipped, and powerfully situated in seats of rule!

Nevertheless, a glorious future is ensured by God's sovereign decree and on His principles, as we shall see, for He "works all things after the counsel of His will."[9] The disciples then and today must learn that Almighty God causes all things, even the evil intentions of man, to work to His own ultimate glory and the good of His redeemed people.[10]

Regarding the greatness of this Great Commission to the nations, our command is not a command to "make bricks without straw." The glorious hope comes "not by might nor by power, but by My Spirit, says the Lord of hosts" (Zech. 4:6b).

---

4. Cp. Matt. 28:16 with 26:56, 69-75.
5. John 19:5-16; 20:19; Acts 4:26-27.
6. Matt. 23:34-36; 24:9-13, 34 (and parallels); Acts 20:28-31; 1 Pet. 1:6-7; 4:12-19.
7. John 19:6, 15; Acts 4:17-18, 33, 7:54—58; 9:1-3; etc.
8. Christ was taunted, scourged, and crucified by the Roman procurator Pontius Pilate, despite Pilate's knowing Christ's innocence (John 18:38; 19:4, 6, 12).
9. Eph. 1:11; Cp. Dan. 4:35; Psa. 115:3; 135:6; Isa. 46:9,10; 55:11.
10. Gen. 50:20; Psa. 76:10; Acts 4:27-28; Rom. 8:28; Eph. 1:22.

We may know that, in fact, we "can do all things through Him who strengthens" us (Phil. 4:13). For "God is able to make all grace abound to you that always having all sufficiency in everything, you may have an abundance for every good deed . . . . He who supplies seed to the sower and bread for food, will supply and multiply your seed for sowing and increase the harvest of your righteousness" (2 Cor. 9:8, 10).

Rather than on a sinful naturalism, then, the prospect of gospel victory is based on a high supernaturalism that involves the powerful, penetrating spiritual influence of the Word of God and of Christ, which alone is "living and active and sharper than any two-edged sword, and piercing as far as the division of soul and spirit, of both joints and marrow, and able to judge the thoughts and intentions of the heart" (Heb. 4:12). In fact, the gospel of Jesus Christ is the very power of God unto salvation, to the Jew first and also the Greek.[11] And the Great Commission well informs the disciples of this.

The Basis for the Hope

I will not treat at length "the basis of hope," for in essence I have done so earlier (Chapter 3-4). But I do need to reintroduce it into my treatment at this juncture by way of reminder. *The sure basis for the glorious hope of mankind's redemption is the sovereign authority of Jesus Christ, the Lord of lords and King of kings.*

We should remember that the Great Commission opened with this noble declaration: "All authority has been given to Me in heaven and on earth" (Matt. 28:18b). That authority encompassed heaven and earth and is "above every name that is named."[12] Christ has the authority to perform His will among men.[13] He has "all authority" to command these frail, fumbling, and fearful disciples to engage the world changing work He wants done. In addition, that authority involves the Triune God, as well, for baptism is in "the name of the Father and the

---

11. Rom. 1:16; 1 Cor. 1:18; 1 Thess. 1:5; 2 Tim. 1:8.
12. Eph. 1:21 Phil. 2:9 Phil. 2:10 1 Pet. 3:22.
13. Acts 18:9-10; Rom. 9:19; 2 Tim. 4:17; Rev. 19:11-16.

Son and the Holy Spirit" (Matt. 28:19b). What are the powers
of mortal men or even of infernal Hell against such authority?

The Power for the Hope

By the grace of God — and only by the grace of God — are
we enabled to do the work of the Lord with the hope of success: "Therefore, my beloved brethren, be steadfast, immovable,
always abounding in the work of the Lord, knowing that your
toil is not in vain *in the Lord*" (1 Cor. 15:58b). Though weak in
and of ourselves, we are promised that Christ's "grace is sufficient for you, for power is perfected in weakness" (2 Cor.
12:9a). *His* power is perfected in *our* weakness. The assurance
of covenantal succesion via the Great Commission is granted
with these truths in mind.

The words of authority claimed by Christ throw the emphasis squarely on Him to whom the authority was given. The
exact order of words in Christ's opening statement in the Commission is: "Given to me was all authority in heaven and on
earth."[14] Grammatically, words cast forward in Greek sentences receive emphasis (this is called "prolepsis"); here those emphasized words are: "given *to me*." Standing there before and
with them in His resurrection body was the very One Who had
just conquered death itself! As He opened His mouth to them
He declared that He had the authority necessary for their aid.
His very presence was an object lesson: He has authority to do
the unthinkable.[15]

Furthermore, though He would be returning bodily to heav-
en soon (Acts 1:9), He left an enabling promise with them:
"And lo, I am with you always, even to the end of the age"
(Matt. 28:20b). Not only does He arrest their attention with this

---

14. Robert Young, *Young's Literal Translation of the Holy Bible* (3rd ed.: Grand Rapids:
Baker, n.d. [1898]), New Testament, p. 23.

15. There is an absurd liberal theory of Christ's death and resurrection called the
"Swoon Theory." This theory teaches that Christ passed out from exhaustion on the
cross and was revived by the coolness of the tomb. In that His treatment was so severe,
however, He could have had no influence on the disciples in a battered body from which
He claimed "all authority in heaven and earth."

attention focusing "lo," but again the Greek syntax is instructive. The Greek language is an inflected language. That is, its verbs do not require pronouns to specify their meaning. Contained in the verb ending itself is the pronoun idea. But when pronouns are used with the verb, as here, much emphasis is being cast on the statement. As Robertson puts it: "When the nominative pronoun is expressed, there is a certain amount of emphasis for the subject is in the verb already."[16]

In the Greek, Christ could have said merely: "I am with you" (Gk: *meth humon eimi*). But He is much more emphatic; He is determined to drive the point home to these frail disciples. Here He says literally: "I with you I am" (Gk: *ego meth humon eimi*). As Lenski notes: "*Ego* is decidedly emphatic," meaning essentially: " 'I myself.' " That is, paraphrasing this into English phraseology, He says: "I myself am with you." The drift is obvious: His scattered, fearful disciples should "let their eyes and their hearts remain fixed on him."[17] He who claims "all authority in heaven and earth" and who has arisen from the dead will be with them.[18]

Believers are adequately empowered for the task of world evangelism and the Christian culture transforming labor that follows in evangelism's trail.[19] The Christian has the abiding presence of the resurrected Lord of glory[20] through the spiritual operation of the indwelling Holy Spirit,[21] Whom Christ says grants "power from on high" (Luke 24:49). The Christian should not read the newspapers and fear the encroachments of the various branches of secular humanism in history, for secular humanism in all of its manifestations is but an idol for destruction.[22]

---

16. A. T. Robertson and W. Hersey Davis, *A New Short Grammar of the Greek Testament* (10th ed.: Grand Rapids: Baker, 1958), p. 264.

17. Lenski, *Matthew*, p. 1180.

18. Interestingly, Matthew's Gospel opens with Christ's prophetic name "Immanuel," which means "God with us" (Matt. 1:23). He also promises to be with His people in Matt. 18:20.

19. Christ will strengthen His people to do His work, John 16:33; Acts 26:16-18; Phil. 4:13; Rev. 1:9-20.

20. Matt. 18:20; John 14:18; Acts 18:10; Gal. 2:20; Heb. 13:5.

21. John 7:39; 14:16-18; Rom. 8:9; 1 John 4:4.

22 Herbert Schlossberg, *Idols for Destruction: Christian Faith and Its Confrontation with*

The Permanence of the Hope

And this powerful, enabling presence is not limited to the apostolic era of the Church. For the fourth time in these three verses He speaks of "all." In verse 18 He claimed "all authority." In verse 19 He commanded the discipling of "all the nations." In verse 20a, He commanded the observing of "all whatever He commanded." In verse 20b, He promised "I am with you 'all the days'[23] — til the full end of the age."[24]

Here Christ's promise is a covenantal promise establishing succession arrangements. His perpetual presence will be with His people for however long they are upon the earth. The grammar here suggests He will be with them *each and every day*, through "all the days" that come their way. And due to the magnitude of the work before them — He commanded them to "disciple *all* the nations" — His Second Advent, which will close the gospel age, necessarily lays off in the distant future. As Bruce perceptively observes: "all the days, of which, it is implied, there may be many; the vista of the future is lengthening."[25] Nevertheless, the resurrected Christ promises, "I myself" with "all authority in heaven and earth" am with you until that distant end.

The Commission's Goal

I have shown that by establishing the succession of the covenant, the powerful Christ promises to be with His people always. But this only renders the glorious prospect of world con-

---

American Society (Nashville: Thomas Nelson, 1983).
   23. The Greek here translated literally is: *pasas tas hemeras*, "all the days."
   24. Young, *Literal Translation*, New Testament p. 23.
   25. A. B. Bruce, *Englishman's Greek Testament* (Grand Rapids: Wm. B. Eerdmans, rep. 1980 [n.d.]), 1:340. See the expectation of a long period of time between the First and Second Advents of Christ in Matt. 21:33; 24:48 25:14, 19; Mark 12:1; Luke 12:45; 19:12; 20:9; 2 Pet. 3:4-9; Luke 12:45. For a helpful article on the anticipated delay in the Second Advent of Christ, we refer the reader once again to: Herbert W. Bowsher, "Will Christ Return 'At Any Moment'?", *The Journal of Christian Reconstruction* 7:2 (Winter, 1981), 48-60. See also: Greg L. Bahnsen and Kenneth L. Gentry, Jr., *House Divided: The Break-up of Dispensational Theology* (Tyler, TX: Institute for Christian Economics, 1989), pp. 217-222.

version and the glorious future resultant from that a theoretical
possibility. With Christ's presence the magnitude of the job certainly is not overwhelming.

But shall it come to pass in *actuality*? Is the evangelization of
the entire world — including virtually all men and nations —
the anticipated goal of the Great Commission? In an important
sense, we are inquiring into the correspondence between the
Lord's Prayer and the Great Commission: Are we believingly to
pray "Thy kingdom come, thy will be done on earth as it is in
heaven" (Matt. 6:10) and then to labor actually to fulfill the
Commission to "make disciples of all the nations"?

Was John Calvin (1509-1564) correct long ago when he
wrote the following regarding Christ and the Great Commission?

> He had to hold supreme and truly divine power of command, to
> declare that eternal life was promised in His name, that the whole
> globe was held under His sway, and that a doctrine was published
> which would subdue all high-seeking, and bring the whole human
> race to humility.[26]

> Briefly, they were to lead all nations into the obedience of faith by
> publishing the Gospel everywhere and that they should seal and
> certify their teaching by the mark of the Gospel.[27]

Was the beloved commentator Matthew Henry (1662-1714) in
line with biblical warrant when he paraphrased Christ's command in the Great Commission as follows: "Do your utmost to
make the nations Christian nations"?[28]

It seems indisputable that this is precisely what Christ anticipates here. Let us carefully note how this is so.

The Hope Affirmed

Earlier in Chapter 4, I noted how Christ directed the Com-

---

26. John Calvin, *Harmony*, p. 249.
27. *Ibid.*, p. 250.
28. Matthew Henry, *Matthew Henry's Commentary on the Whole Bible* (Old Tappan, NJ:
Fleming H. Revell, n.d. [1721]) 5:446.

mission to all cultures and nations, and not just to individuals. In Chapter 5 I showed how the mission of Christ's people was to "disciple" those to whom it was directed. Here I take a step further to consider the important fact that Christ fully expects that the nations will be converted and brought under His gracious sway.

Again I must qualify what I am saying in order to dispel any erroneous perceptions. I am *not* saying that the sum total of the Great Commission is directed to cultural renewal and that all else is incidental. *The initial influence of the Great Commission necessarily works first in individuals, saving them from their sins and giving them new hearts.* Then, those individuals who are saved and have been given new hearts are obligated to live new lives. To all Christians the Scriptures command that you are to "work out your salvation with fear and trembling; for it is God who is at work in you, both to will and to work for His good pleasure" (Phil. 2:12b-13). Christians are to bring every thought captive to the obedience to Christ (2 Cor. 10:5). Christian cultural transformation necessarily demands the wide-scale salvation of multitudes of individuals. Implied in Christian cultural renewal is individual personal salvation.[29]

Having briefly noted that, I now turn to the words of the Great Commission as actually uttered by our Lord. The relevant portion of Christ's command is really quite clear: "*disciple all the nations, baptizing them in the name of the Father and the Son and the Holy Spirit.*" That He fully expects the successful discipling of all the nations, may be supported on the following bases:

First, the grammatical structure of the command expects worldwide conversions. The Greek verb *matheteuo* ("disciple") here is in the active voice and is followed by a noun in the accusative case, *ethne* ("nations"). In addition, it is important to

---

29. Two of the most prolific writers calling for Christian cultural transformation are Rousas J. Rushdoony and Gary North. Yet in Rushdoony's massive *Institutes of Biblical Law*, regeneration is frequently set forth as the pre-condition to success in the endeavor. R. J. Rushdoony, *Institutes of Biblical Law* (Vallecito, CA: Ross House, 1973), pp. 113, 122, 147, 308, 413, 627, 780. In North's works the same holds true. Gary North, *Political Polytheism: The Myth of Plurality* (Tyler, TX: Institute for Christian Economics, 1989), pp. 133, 157, 585-586, 611.

understand that this verb *matheteuo* is "normally an intransitive verb [but is] here used transitively."[30] That is, *matheteuo* transfers its action (discipling) to its direct object (nations). *Matheteuo* appears only two times in the New Testament in the active voice and coupled with an accusative, here and in Acts 14:21.[31] The Acts passage is helpful in understanding the significance of the grammatical structure.

In Acts 14:21 we read: "Having proclaimed good news also to that city, and *having discipled many*, they turned back to Lystra, and Iconium, and Antioch."[32] Here it is evident to all that the "many" have been "discipled." Who would dispute the clear statement that the apostles actually "discipled" (the active voice of *mathetuo*) the "many" expressly mentioned? And this same grammatical relationship appears in Matthew 28:19, where we read the command: *"disciple* all the *nations."* How is it that some do not understand Christ's command to involve the *actual discipling* of "all the nations"? Is not the word "nations" in the accusative case and therefore the direct object of the discipling labor of the Church? In addition, Lenski states of this command to disciple: "this imperative, of course, means 'to turn into disciples,' and its aorist [tense] form conveys the thought that it is actually to be done."[33]

Second, the lexical meaning of the term *matheteuo* supports the teaching of the expectation of worldwide conversions. As I noted earlier in another context, the Greek verb *matheteuo* does not mean merely "to witness." It involves the actual bringing of the person or persons under the authoritative influence and instruction of the one discipling. It entails the actual making of a disciple for Christ.

Third, the supplementary and co-ordinate command anticipates worldwide conversions. It is evident that the command to

---

30. D. A. Carson, "Matthew" in Frank E. Gaebelein, ed., *The Expositor's Bible Commentary* (Grand Rapids: Regency Reference Library, 1984), 8:595.

31. A. T. Robertson, *A Greek Grammar in the Light of Historical Research* (Nashville: Broadman, 1934), p. 475.

32. Robert Young, *Young's Literal Translation of the Holy Bible* (Grand Rapids: Baker, n.d. [1898]), New Testament, p. 94

33. Lenski, *Matthew,* p. 1172.

disciple actually expects the conversion and training of the nations, for those nations are then to be baptized: "make disciples of all the nations, baptizing them" (Gk: *autous*). According to Christ's command, those who are discipled are to be baptized, which action clearly portrays their coming under the authority of the Triune God, i.e., becoming Christians.[34] In the original Greek, the plural pronoun *autous* ("them") refers back to the plural noun *ethne* ("nations"). The *nations* are expected to become Christians by discipleship and to be marked out as under God's rule by baptism.

There are those who attempt to circumvent this point by arguing that the pronoun "them" does not refer back to the "nations," but to those who are made disciples.[35] They suggest that it is not the nations as such, but individuals from among the nations who will be baptized. They do so because the pronoun found here, *autous* ("them") is in the masculine form, whereas the noun *ethne* ("nations") is a neuter noun. Normally pronouns agree in gender with their antecedent nouns. The idea forwarded is that the noun form of the verb "to disciple" is *mathetes*, which is in the masculine gender.

This view does not seem to have sufficient merit, however, for it requires the reading of a noun ("disciple") where a verb ("to disciple") actually appears. And it does so despite there being a suitable antecedent noun present, which is separated from the pronoun by only one word.[36] Also it presses a general rule beyond necessity. Winer's *Grammar* notes: "it is a peculiarity common to the Pronouns, whether personal, demonstrative, or relative, that they not unfrequently take a different gender from that of the nouns to which they refer, regard being had to the *meaning* of the nouns, not to their grammatical sex . . . as Matt. xxviii.19 . . . ."[37] Robertson dogmatically states: "In Mt. 28:19 *autous* refers to *ethne*." He, too, points out

---

34. See discussion of "baptizing in the name" (Matt. 28:19), pp. 81-84.
35. Carson, "Matthew," *EBC* 8:597.
36. The relevant portion of the Greek of Matthew 28:19 is: *matheteusate panta ta ethne, baptizontes autous*, "disciple all the *nations* (*ethne*), baptizing *them* (*autous*).
37. George Benedict Winer, *A Grammar of the Idiom of the New Testament*, rev. by Gottlieb Lunemann (7th ed: Andover: Warren F. Draper, 1886), Sec. 21-2, p. 141.

that "personal pronouns are sometimes used freely according to sense."[38] Lenski concurs.[39] The discipling is of "all the nations" (Matt. 28:19a). The preaching of repentance is to "all the nations" (Luke 24:47). Why should not all the nations be baptized (Matt. 28:19b)? In fact, do not the Old Testament prophets expect such? For example, Isaiah 52:12-15 prophesies of Christ:

> Behold, My servant will prosper,
> He will be high and lifted up,
>   and greatly exalted.
> Just as many were astonished at you, My people,
> So His appearance was marred more than any man,
> And His form more than the sons of men.
> Thus He will *sprinkle many nations*,
> Kings will shut their mouths on account of Him." (Emphasis added.)

Fourth, the eschatology of Scripture elsewhere expects worldwide conversions. Although space prohibits our full discussion of the evidence, I will select just two classes of evidence for the discipling and baptizing — the Christianization — of the world.[40]

The presence and prospects of Christ's kingdom. That Christ's kingdom is powerfully present and growing in influence is evident upon the following points considerations:

1. The *time* of the kingdom came in Christ's ministry: "The time is fulfilled, and the kingdom of God is at hand" (Mark 1:14-15).[41]

---

38. Robertson, *Historical Grammar*, p. 684. He lists the following examples in which the personal pronoun *autos* refers back to non-personal nouns: the "world" (2 Cor. 5:19), a "city" (Acts 8:5), a "crowd" (Mark 6:64), and "the uncircumcised" (Rom. 2:26).

39. Lenski, *Matthew*, p. 1179.

40. For a fuller discussion see: Greg L. Bahnsen and Kenneth L. Gentry, Jr., *House Divided: The Break-up of Dispensational Theology* (Tyler, TX: Institute for Christian Economics, 1989), pp. 139-286. See also: Roderick Campbell, *Israel and the New Covenant* (Tyler, TX: Geneva Divinity School Press, 1983 [1954]); David Chilton, *Paradise Restored* (Ft. Worth: Dominion, 1985); John Jefferson Davis, *Christ's Victorious Kingdom: Postmillennialism Reconsidered* (Grand Rapids: Baker, 1986). Consult also the systematic theologies by Charles Hodge, A. A. Hodge, W. G. T. Shedd, and Robert L. Dabney.

41. See also: Matt. 3:2; 4:17. Cp. Luke 4:16-21; Gal. 4:4; 2 Cor. 6:2.

2. The kingdom was declared present and operative during His ministry: "If I cast out demons by the Spirit of God, then the kingdom of God has come upon you" (Matt. 12:28).[42]

3. In the lifetime of His hearers it would show its power: "Truly I say to you, there are some of those who are standing here who shall not taste of death until they see the kingdom of God after it has come with power" (Mark 9:1).[43]

4. Christ is even now at the throne of God ruling and reigning over His kingdom: "He who overcomes, I will grant to him to sit down with Me on My throne, as I also overcame and sat down with My Father on His throne" (Rev. 3:22).[44]

5. His rule will grow to encompass the entire world until He has put down all opposition: "He, having offered one sacrifice for sins for all time, sat down at the right hand of God, waiting from that time onward until His enemies be made a footstool for His feet" (Heb. 10:12-13).[45]

The design and results of Christ's redemption. It is evident from the New Testament record that Christ's design in salvation was to secure the redemption of the world, as I showed earlier.[46]

1. He died in order to redeem the "world." The Greek word for "world" (*kosmos*) signifies the world as the system of men and things. God created this world of men and things; Christ has come to redeem it back to God. "God did not send the Son into the world to judge the world; but that the world should be saved through Him" (John 3:17).[47]

---

42. See also: Matt. 11:11-14; 12:28; Luke 11:20; 16:16; 17:20-21.

43. See also: Matt. 16:18, 19; 26:64.

44. Acts 2:29-36; Rom. 8:34; Eph. 1:20-23; Phil. 2:8-11; Heb. 1:3, 13; 1 Pet. 3:22; Rev. 1:5-6.

45. See also: Matt. 13:31-33; 1 Cor. 15:20-26; Heb. 1:13; 10:12-13. Hal Lindsey disputes the use of Matt. 13:33 in this connection: Some "try to make the symbol of *leaven* in this parable refer to the kingdom of God and how it will spread to take dominion over the earth. However, there's one big problem with that interpretation — *leaven* in the Bible *is always used as a symbol of evil's explosive power to spread.* It is never used as a symbol of good." Lindsey, *Holocaust*, p. 47. However, there are *three* "big problems" with Lindsey's interpretation: (1) Leaven does not *explode*; it works slowly and subtly. (2) It is used in some offerings to God in the Old Testament and surely does not represent an evil gift to God (Lev. 7:13 and 23:7). (3) It is absurd to say that Christ preached "the kingdom of heaven is like *evil* (leaven)!

46. See pages 55-58, for a fuller exposition of these points.

47. See also: John 1:29; 1 John 2:2; 4:14; 2 Cor. 5:19. See: B. B. Warfield, "Christ

2. He died with the expectation of drawing "all men" to Himself: "I, if I be lifted up from the earth, will draw all men to Myself" (John 12:31).[48] Christ is called "the Savior of the world," because of the comprehensive design and massive influence of His redemptive labors. The Great Commission is the means by which God will draw all men to Christ.

The Hope Denied

Despite the clear statement in the Great Commission, there are evangelical Christians of influence who somehow miss what seems so obvious. At an academic discussion held over this whole question, some evangelicals maintained "the futility of trying to change the world in the current age."[49] Dispensational theologian Harold Hoehner replied against the postmillennial hope: "I just can't buy their basic presupposition that we can do anything significant to change the world."[50]

Another evangelical, Albert Dager, has stated: "To 'disciple all the nations,' or, 'make disciples [out of] all the nations,' does not mean that every nation as a whole is one day going to . . . learn the ways of Truth. The Great Commission requires us to go into all the nations and disciple 'whosoever will' be saved."[51] It is interesting to note that in order to discount the glorious expectation of the Commission, Dager has to import words into the text. The following italicized words show his textual additions: "make disciples [*out* of] all the nations," "go *into* all the nations" and "disciple '*whosoever will*.'" Christ simply says: "make disciples of all the nations," without all the embellishments. The basic issue is this: discipling (disciplining) nations means *extending God's kingdom authority in history.*

---

the Propitiation for the Sins of the World," ed. by John E. Meeter, in *The Selected Shorter Writings of Benjamin B. Warfield* (Nutley, NJ: Presbyterian and Reformed, 1970 [1915]), 1:23.
    48. See also: 1 Tim. 2:6.
    49. Cited by Randy Frame, "Is Christ or Satan Ruler of This World?" *Christianity Today*, 34:4 (March 5, 1990) 42.
    50. *Ibid.*, p. 43.
    51. Albert James Dager, "Kingdom Theology: Part III," *Media Spotlight* (January-June, 1987), p. 11.

One recent evangelical book attempts a strong case against the obvious meaning of the Great Commission, a case which forms, in essence, the whole point of that book. Popular writer Hal Lindsey vigorously assaults the very interpretation of the Great Commission, which I am suggesting. He cites the Great Commission with translational observations and then comments on those observations: "Go therefore and make disciples of [Greek=*out of*] all the nations [*ta ethne* in Greek=*the Gentiles*], baptizing them . . . . Nothing in these great commission passages implies that we will convert the world and take dominion over it."[52]

Later, after citing postmillennialists who view the Commission as I am presenting it, he comments:

> They interpret the command "make disciples of all the nations" to mean the Christianizing of society and culture, and the systematic taking over of all the governments[53] of the world.
> There is a very important reason, in addition to those listed above, why this interpretation is unsupportable from the Bible. The original Greek text of Matthew 28:19 will not permit this interpretation. The genitive construction means "a part out of a whole." The term "nations" is the same Greek word (*ethne*) I dealt with in chapter four . . . .
> There never has been and there never will be a totally Christian nation *until* the Lord Jesus Christ personally reigns upon this earth.[54]

In response, I say there is a very important reason why Lindsey's interpretation is unsupportable: There is absolutely *no genitive* case "nations" in Matthew 28:19! If there is no genitive, there can be no "genitive construction." What he thinks is the genitive case is actually an accusative, with which he accuses us!

---

52. Hal Lindsey, *The Road to Holocaust* (New York: Bantam, 1989), p. 49 (emphasis his).

53. His statement goes a little too far here with the somewhat extreme sounding embellishment: "systematic taking over of all the governments of the world." This sounds militaristic and revolutionary — especially since his book opens with a quotation from Adolf Hitler! Our view is of the gracious and redemptive victory of Christ's gospel over men and nations, not armed revolution.

54. *Ibid.*, p. 277.

Consequently, his very "important reason" is a figment of his imagination. Furthermore, the Scriptures I have cited above do expect a Christian world as a result of the promotion of the Gospel of Jesus Christ.

Donald G. Barnhouse, a dispensationalist forerunner of Lindsey, Hunt, and others cited herein, is surely wrong when he presses the point of a perpetual minority status for Christianity. He attempts to do so based on the statement in Acts 15:14: "So, together, they mean 'to call out of,' to take something out of its setting. This is what God does. He reaches down and takes out a people. God is not going to save everyone in Philadelphia, or New York, or San Francisco, or Rocktown Center, or wherever. No, God says, 'I'm saving this one, and that one, and these, and those and this person and that individual.'"[55]

But then, what becomes of His being the Savior of the *world* (John 4:42) and of *all men* (John 12:32)? Why does He command us to "disciple *all nations*, baptizing them" (Matt. 28:19)?

House and Ice assert of the various post-resurrection commissions of Christ: "there is no language or tone in either of these passages that would support the notion of Christianizing the world."[56] But as I have shown, that is precisely the "language" and "tone" of the Great Commission. It is interesting that these dispensationalist[57] writers are at variance with other dispensationalists, who vehemently argue that the Great Commission *does* involve the very discipling of the nations. Dispensationalist W. H. Griffith Thomas writes:

English phrase, "make disciples of all the nations," is ambiguous, for literal rendering of Greek is, rather, "make all nations disciples" and not "make disciples out of all nations"; thus, commission embraces whole nations rather than indicating individuals from among them (cf. Acts 14:21, which means that apostles "made many people

---

55. Donald Grey Barnhouse, *Acts: An Expositional Commentary* (Grand Rapids: Zondervan, 1979), p. 137.
56. H. Wayne House and Thomas D. Ice, *Dominion Theology: Blessing or Curse?* (Portland, OR: Multnomah, 1988), p. 152.
57. For a definition of "dispensationalism," see Chapter 11.

disciples") . . . .

Matthew gives aim and scope of Great Commission, and passages like Acts 14:21 and 15:14 actual results.[58]

Neither are amillennialists[59] immune from washing out the victory inherent in the Great Commission and elsewhere in Scripture. An otherwise excellent treatise entitled *God-Centered Evangelism* by reformed theologian R. B. Kuiper sees no ultimate pre-Second Advent victory for the Great Commission: "Jesus' parables of the mustard seed and the leaven (Matt. 13:31-33) teach the growth of Christ's kingdom; and the growth of Satan's kingdom is patently implicit in the Saviour's plaintive query: 'When the Son of man cometh, shall he find faith on the earth?' That twofold process [of the concurrent growth of Christ's kingdom and Satan's kingdom] is being exemplified in current events. The heathen nations are slowly being Christianized, while the Christian nations are reverting to paganism."[60]

Likewise, Anthony Hoekema writes: "[A]longside of the growth and development of the kingdom of God in the history of the world since the coming of Christ we also see the growth and development of the kingdom of evil."[61] And in response to the postmillennial interpretation of Matthew 28:18-20 as set forth by Loraine Boettner,[62] Hoekema argues: "The clear implication of [Matthew 13:36-43] is that Satan's kingdom, if we may call it that, will continue to exist and grow as long as God's kingdom grows, until Christ comes again. The New Testament gives indications of the continuing strength of that 'kingdom of evil until the end of the world.'"[63] Hendrikus Berkhof also pos-

58. W. H. Griffith Thomas, *Outline Studies in the Gospel of Matthew* (Grand Rapids: Eerdmans, 1961), pp. 464, 465.

59. For a definition of "amillennialism," see Chapter 11.

60. R. B. Kuiper, *God-Centered Evangelism* (Grand Rapids: Baker, 1961), p. 209.

61. Anthony Hoekema, *The Bible and the Future* (Grand Rapids: Wm. B. Eerdmans, 1979), p. 35 (cp. 68, 70n, 118-119, 134, 136).

62. *Ibid.*, p. 177.

63. *Ibid.*, p. 180.

its a parallel development of good and evil.[64]

Conclusion

We must ask ourselves important questions regarding the expectation of the Great Commission. For instance, since the Great Commission is a covenantal obligation, does it not have appropriate succession arrangements, which are designed to insure its continuance and fulfillment? We should consider which is stronger, sinful depravity or gracious redemption?[65] Is not the gospel "the power of God unto salvation" (Rom. 1:16)? Does Satan have an equally great commission? Is Christ struggling to a draw until the last moments of history? Shall Antichrist prevail in the very history in which Christ entered and commissioned His Church?[66]

All such non-postmillennial thinking runs aground on the very greatness of the Great Commission. For in that Commission we find a vivid expectation of a gospel-induced conversion of the world. An expectation fully compatible with the teaching of Scripture in all sections. An anticipation that does not require a reading of words into the text. A glorious hope that is fully commensurate with the authority available and the goal set.

---

64. Hendrikus Berkhof, *Christ the Meaning of History*, trans. from the 4th ed., by L. Buurman (Grand Rapids: Baker, 1979 [1966]), p.p 177-178.

65. Ask yourself the following: Have any lost people ever been saved? Then ask: Have any saved ever been lost? Now compare the answers to determine which is stronger, grace or sin.

66. See Norman Shepherd, "Justice to Victory" in *The Journal of Christian Reconstruction* 3:3 (Winter, 1976-77) 6-10.

Part III

APPLICATIONS

8

THE CHURCH AND
THE GREAT COMMISSION

And He put all things under His feet, and gave Him to be head over all things to the church which is His body, the fullness of Him who fills all in all (Ephesians 1:22-23).

As I pointed out earlier, all theological and biblical truth necessarily has practical implications. The Bible is God's Word given to direct us in the paths of righteousness.[1] In the Christian life, theory is foundational to practice. Or to put it in biblical terms, truth is foundational to sanctification: "Sanctify them in the truth; Thy word is truth" (John 17:17).

God has ordained three basic institutions in society: the the Church, the family, and the State.[2] A biblical understanding of their respective roles and inter-relationships is fundamental to developing a Christian worldview. The fulfilling of the Great Commission in history will require not only a proper *understanding* of each of these institutions, but also concerned *involvement* in each.

I now turn briefly to consider a few practical directives for promoting the truths contained in the Commission. What, then, are some initial, practical applications of the Great Commission for each of the three fundamental institutions? In this chapter,

---

1. Psa. 119:105; Isa. 2:3; Matt. 7:24; Jms. 1:22.
2. See: Gary North, *The Sinai Strategy: Economics and the Ten Commandments* (Tyler, TX: Institute for Christian Economics, 1986), ch. 3: "Oaths, Covenants, and Contracts."

I will focus on the Church.

In 1981 the Association of Reformation Churches published a proposed additional chapter to its confessional statement. That chapter was entitled "Of the Christian Mission." Paragraph 4 of that revision reads:

> As a ministry of worship, the mission of the church is to organize the communal praise of the saints. As a ministry of redemptive grace, the church has been given the mission of calling men back into full fellowship with the Creator. The church proclaims the Word of God. To those outside the Kingdom, she calls for repentance and faith in Christ Jesus. To those within, she calls for obedience and growth in grace in every sphere of life. While the church must not usurp the duties of state and family, she must witness prophetically to those laboring in those institutions, calling on them in the Name of God to conform their labors to the requirements of Scripture. . . .
>
> Since Christ has promised to His Kingdom a glorious future, when all nations will flow to the house of the Lord, the growth of the church is usually to be expected. This growth, however. is to be accomplished not through any means which may come to hand, but only through means which are consonant with Holy Scripture.[3]

The Problem We Face

With all the recent negative publicity regarding the misdeeds of certain televangelists and the theological distortions by others, the Church of Jesus Christ is suffering a credibility and integrity crisis.[4] But defection from church attendance did not begin in the late 1980s with those errant men. It has for a number of decades been a problem in America.

Church is seen as optional to the Christian life by too many Christians today. Many who profess to be Christians know too little of devoted commitment to Christ.[5] They seem oblivious to

---

3. "Of the Christian Mission" in *The Failure of the American Baptist Culture*, vol. 1 of *Christianity and Civilization* (Tyler, TX: Geneva Divinity School, 1982), pp. 95-96.

4. Mike Horton, ed., *The Agony of Deceit: What Some TV Preachers Are Really Teaching* (Chicago: Moody, 1990). James R. Goff, Jr., "The Faith that Claims," *Christianity Today* 34:3 (February 19, 1990) 18-21.

5. Ryrie is concerned over Lordship doctrine as taught by John MacArthur, myself, and others, when he asks: "where is there room for carnal Christians?" Charles C. Ryrie,

the demands of the Great Commission regarding discipleship. What, then, should be the Christian's approach to church life, as he submits himself to Christ under the Great Commission?

Principles of the Covenantal Church

1. *Commitment to the local church.* A major and indispensable aspect of our commitment to Christ involves our membership in, attendance at, worship in, and service through the local church. Church attendance and membership is expected and obligated on several grounds: (a) Christ established the Church as a part of His ongoing plan for His people.[6] (b) Christ died for His Church, evidencing a great love and concern for it.[7] (c) The Church is the central place God has ordained for Christian fellowship and service.[8] (d) Church attendance puts us under the ministry of doctrine for our spiritual growth.[9] (e) Christ has ordained church officers to govern His people.[10] (f) Christ has given spiritual disciplinary power to the officers of the Church for the good of His people.[11] (g) God has given the sacraments only to the Church.[12] The Lord's Supper specifically is designated for the corporate communing among God's people.[13] (h) God clearly commands us not to forsake attending church.[14]

2. *Engagement to worship.* Christ expects His people to worship Him in spirit and in truth (John 4:24), corporately in the fellowship of God's people.[15]

Balancing the Christian Life (Chicago: Moody, 1969), p. 170. See: John F. MacArthur, Jr., *The Gospel According to Jesus* (Grand Rapids: Zondervan, 1988) and Kenneth L. Gentry, Jr., "The Great Option: A Study of the Lordship Controversy," *Baptist Reformation Review* 5:52 (Spring, 1976), pp. 40ff.

6. Matt. 16:18; Acts 20:28; Eph. 2:19-22; 1 Pet. 2:5-9.

7. John 15:10; Acts 20:29; Eph. 5:25.

8. Acts 2:42; Rom. 12:3-16; 1 Cor. 12:13ff; Gal. 6:1-6.

9. Eph. 4:11-14; 1 Tim. 4:13; 1 Pet. 2:1-3.

10. Acts 6:1-6; 13:1-3; 15:1-32; 20:28; 1 Tim. 3:1-13; Tit. 1:1-9; 1 Pet. 5:1-5.

11. Matt. 18:15-20; 1 Cor. 5:1-5; 1 Thess. 5:13-14; Heb. 13:17.

12. Matt. 28:18-19; Acts 20:7; 1 Cor. 11:23ff.

13. Acts 20:7; 1 Cor. 10:16-17; 11:20-34.

14. Heb. 10:24,25; 1 Cor. 12:12-25. See the symbolism of systemic unity in John 15:1ff; Eph. 2:19-22; 1 Pet. 2:5-9.

15. Acts 1:14; 2:42; Deut. 12:32; Acts 17:25; See also: Paul E. Engle, *Discovering the*

Worship is man's highest calling. It is to be both generic and specific. That is, worship is to be engaged in every day life,[16] as well as in specific, formal exercise on the Lord's Day.[17] The various elements of Christian worship are to be engaged with the whole heart, soul, mind, and strength (Mark 12:30), not while asleep, in a trance, or fidgeting while wondering about lunch. The manner of worship is legislated by God in Scripture; we must approach the Covenant God on His terms (e.g., Lev. 10:1,2). Hymns, prayers, offerings, exhortations, confessions, Scripture readings, sermons, and other aspects of worship are not to be performed by mere rote reflex. They are to be engaged with devotion, as unto the Lord. In other words, we must remember that Christ is with us "all the days" (Matt. 28:20, Gk.) — including while we worship. We are to rejoice in the baptism of new converts, as an aspect of our worship and as we witness the discipling of the nations (Matt. 28:19).

3. *Training in the truth.* The Christian should seek a church that promotes sound doctrine and the development of a Christian worldview based on biblical teaching.

The church should be a covenant-community fellowship, committed to the historic creeds of the Christian faith (the Apostles' Creed, Nicene Creed, etc.).[18] It should not be associated with the National or World Council of Churches. It should have a solid educational program.

The piecemeal Christian faith so widespread today does not measure up to the calling of discipling toward a Christian culture (Matt. 28:19). The church should actively train people to submit to Christ's authority (Matt. 28:18) and work (Matt. 28:19-20). As a leading officer in the Church, Paul was concerned to promote "the whole counsel of God" (Acts 20:27).

Several programs could be used to promote education in the truth.[19] These include: catechetical training, a church library,

---

Fullness of Worship (Philadelphia: Great Commission Publications, 1978).

16. Rom. 12:1-2; 1 Cor. 10:31.

17. Acts 20:7; 1 Cor. 11: 26; Heb. 10:25.

18. See: R. J. Rushdoony, *The Foundations of Social Order: Studies in the Creeds and Councils of the Early Church* (Fairfax, VA: Thoburn, 1968) and Kenneth L. Gentry, Jr., *The Usefulness of Creeds* (Mauldin, SC: GoodBirth, 1980).

19. An excellent resource and idea book is Gary North, *Backward, Christian Soldiers?*

a small group book-of-the-month fellowship and discussion program,[20] a local theological seminary program for members and the community,[21] and either the setting up of or the supporting of an already established Christian day school.[22]

4. *Training in hierarchical covenantalism.* The church is to be composed of a system of courts designed to locate responsibility and resolve problems, as Christ's people have His authority ministered to them.

The influences of the democratic spirit and of voluntarism are alive and well in American Christianity. And this is unfortunate. The Church of the Lord Jesus Christ is viewed by many as so many islands in the stream of history, unconnected and unconnectable. Bold claims to independency are proudly displayed on thousands of church signs across the land.

Yet the Scripture has ordained a covenantal government of elected hierarchical rule in the church — a rule patterned on the Old Testament revelation (Exo. 18:19-23; Deut. 1:13-15). In the Old Testament, elders possessed jurisdictional authority (Exo. 12:21, cp. v. 3)[23] and were organized into graduated levels of courts (Deut. 1:15). The New Testament office of rulership in the Church even adopts the same name as the Old Testament office: elder (1 Tim. 3:1ff).[24]

We need to teach our churches of the divinely ordained system of covenantal government in the Church. In the New Testament Church, each church was to have a plurarlity of elders (Acts 14:23; Tit. 1:5). New Testament elders are vested with real governmental authority not exercised by the congregation at large, as the following indicate: (1) Though Christ

---

An Action Manual for Christian Reconstruction (Tyler, TX: Institute for Christian Economics, 1984).

20. It might be profitable to have participants read: Mortimer Adler and Charles Van Doren, *How To Read a Book* (rev. ed.; New York: Simon and Schuster, 1972 [1939]).

21. Whitefield Theological Seminary (P. O. Box 6321, Lakeland, Florida 33807), has a program that is designed to operate in local communities.

22. Robert Thoburn, *How to Establish and Operate a Successful Christian School* (Fairfax, VA: Thoburn, 1975).

23. See also: Num. 35:12, 24 (cp. Josh. 20:4); 2 Sam. 5:3 (cp. v. 1).

24. "Elder" appears 100 times in the Old Testament and thirty-one times in the New Testament.

116   THE GREATNESS OF THE GREAT COMMISSION

ultimately "builds" His Church, He gave its keys to men to exercise "binding" authority (Matt. 16:18-19). (2) There is a gift of government given to some, not all Christians (Rom. 12:6-8; 1 Cor. 12:28). (3) Titles expressive of authoritative power are given to some, not all Christians (1 Tim. 3:1,2,6; 5:19). (4) Office is granted by divine appointment and entered by solemn rite; it is not automatic with conversion (1 Tim. 4:14; 5:22). (5) The functions of office are expressive of real authority (Acts 20:28).[25]

This hierarchical authority is graduated into lower and higher courts having authority over individual and multiple congregations. The classic illustration of this is found in Acts 15. There we discover the Church functioning hierarchically to resolve a doctrinal dispute in a particular church at Antioch (Acts 15:1,2). The matter was sent by representatives to a trial before a joint council in Jerusalem (Acts 15:2). The matter was debated before the entire council (Acts 15:4-19).[26] The conclusion of this non-local court action was sent back down to the court of original jurisdiction (Acts 15:20-23). It was considered binding upon the Antiochian church (Acts 15:28) and was sent to other churches for their instruction (Acts 16:4).

Discipling in regard to the nature and structure of church government is important for the vitality of the Christian faith in itself. What is more, the divinely ordained government of the Church is to be a model for the civil government, as well (Deut. 4:5-8).

5. *Promotion of Christ's cause.* In that the church is commanded to go into the world (Matt. 28:19a), it should do so in the name of the Triune God (Matt. 28:19b).

There are a number of opportunities for local evangelistic outreach for the church: friendship evangelism, Bible conferences/seminars, radio and/or television ministry, tape ministry, campus outreach, newsletter ministry,[27] and more. Contrary to

25. See also: 1 Tim. 3:5; 5:17; 1 Pet. 5:1,2.
26. Notice that although apostles were present, they chose not to close the matter by direct apostolic authority. Rather, they encouraged the appeals process.
27. Newsletters should be informative, promotional, and Christ glorifying. They can be used as promotional tools by sending them to new area residents. Two computerized

much church growth advocacy, however, these should be employed to diffuse light (Matt. 5:14), not to entertain the carnal masses.[28]

In friendship evangelism, for instance, the church is to engage its members in evangelistic outreach through one of the most natural and successful means of evangelism: friendship associations through personal acquaintances and family members.[29] Statistically it is reported that the average Christian knows 8.4 unchurched individuals.[30] These are prime targets for friendly overtures by Christians. Furthermore, most Christians today can trace their initial point of contact with Christ through friends and families.[31]

The friendship evangelism methodology is really quite simple. In special training sessions, the church should have each member jot down the names of unchurched acquaintances. These names should be made the matter of specific, long term prayer. A few of these names should be especially set apart by each individual for the purpose of building bridges, i.e. nurturing friendship ties by various means. The ultimate goal of these strengthened ties should be eventually to confront them with the gospel claims either directly or by merely inviting to take them to church with you.

6. *Service in the world.* Although the Church is not *of* the world, it is *in* it and must make her presence felt as "salt" in the earth (Matt. 5:13).

This will involve organizing a truly functional diaconal ministry of social concern and outreach in the name of Christ.

---

mail services that publish regular update lists of new residents moving into any zip code area are: COR Information, 430 Oakmears Crescent, Virginia Beach, VA 23462 and GGC Associates, Inc., 2900 Bristol Street, Suite H-203, Costa Mesa, CA 92626.

28. See Conclusion.

29. See its use among family members, friends, neighbors, employer-employee relationships, and so forth, in: Matt. 9:9-13; Luke 15:3-6, 8-9; John 1:40-45; Acts 10:1-2, 22-24; 16:12-15, 23-31.

30. Jerry W. Lynn, *Sowing Upon the Good Soil* (Clinton, SC: Calvary Presbytery, 1990), p. 3.

31. Lynn's survey statistics indicate the following percentages for getting people into churches: Pastoral influence (3-6%), Sunday school program (4-5%), special needs (3-4%), crusades or revivals (.001%), visitation program (3-6%), special programs (2-5%), and friendship/family overtures (75+%).

Again, this promotes a biblical model for social concern and Christian culture building (Matt. 28:19).[32]

Also the Church should pray about and study social and political issues and encourage social/political involvement through letter writing campaigns and other means.[33] Of course, there is a need to be careful not to endorse candidates and become too "political."[34] In America's colonial history, the Church played an important role as a source of direction and information regarding social and civil affairs. Unfortunately, the Church today is too often a study in irrelevance. Yet Christ calls His Church to be "the light of the world" and "the salt of the earth" (Matt. 5:13-14). Hence, Paul's appointment to take the gospel to nations and kings (Acts 9:15).

---

32. The following books by George Grant are excellent resources: *Bringing in the Sheaves: Transforming Poverty into Productivity* (Atlanta, GA: American Vision, 1985); *The Dispossessed: Homelessness in America* (Ft. Worth, TX: Dominion, 1986); and *In the Shadow of Plenty: Biblical Principles of Welfare and Poverty* (Nashville: Thomas Nelson, 1986). Also see: Gerard Berghoef and Lester De Koster, *The Deacons Handbook: A Manual of Stewardship* (Grand Rapids, MI: Christian's Library Press, 1980) and Leonard J. Coppes, *Who Will Lead Us? A Study in the Development of Biblical Offices with Emphasis on the Diaconate* (Phillipsburg, NJ: Pilgrim, 1977).

33. For several resources of socio-political issues of Christian concern, see: Kenneth L. Gentry, Jr., *The Christian Case Against Abortion* (2nd ed.: Memphis, TN: Footstool, 1990) (abortion morality). *Journal of the American Family Association*, P. O. Drawer 2440, Tupelo, MS 38802 (pornography). *Candidates Biblical Scoreboard*, P. O. Box 10428, Costa Mesa, CA 92627 (political candidates). *A Letterwriter's Guide to Congress*, Chamber of Commerce of the United States, 1615 H St. N. W., Washington, CD 20002 (letter writing campaigns). *Remnant Review*, P. O. Box 8204, Ft. Worth, TX, 76124 (economic/social issues). Rutherford Institute Report, P. O. Box 5101, Manassas, VA, 22110 (legal issues). Franky Schaeffer, *A Time for Anger: The Myth of Neutrality* (Westchester, IL: Crossway, 1982).

34. George Grant, *The Changing of the Guard: Biblical Principles for Political Action* (Ft. Worth: Dominion, 1987); Lynn Buzzard and Paula Campbell, *Holy Disobedience: When Christians Must Resist the State* (Ann Arbor, MI: Servant Books, 1984). Robert L. Thoburn, *The Christian and Politics* (Tyler, TX: Thoburn Press, 1984).

9

THE FAMILY AND
THE GREAT COMMISSION

"Honor your father and mother," which is the first commandment with promise: "that it may be well with you and you may live long on the earth" (Ephesians 6:2-3).

We begin again with the Association of Reformation Churches confessional revision for direction. In paragraph 6 the family is dealt with:

> As a ministry of nurture, the mission of the family is to be the first church and state to the child, rearing him in terms of the grace and law of God the Father. Where the family is broken, the church must be father to the orphan and husband to the widow. Since the child has been committed by God to the parents for nurture, the education of the child is the mission not of the church, nor of the state, but of the family. Where this ministry is delegated to specialists, it must be done so freely, not of coercion.
>
> As a ministry of dominion, the family has been given the cultural mandate as its mission. For the performance of this task, God has given the privilege of private ownership of property to the family. As a result of the sin of man, the work of the cultural mandate not only consists of the acquisition of scientific knowledge and the aesthetic beautification of the environment, but also entails the acquisition of the basic necessities of life.[1]

---

1. "Of the Christian Mission" in *The Failure of the American Baptist Culture*, vol. 1 of *Christianity and Civilization* (Tyler, TX: Geneva Divinity School, 1982), pp. 96-97.

Erosion of the Covenantal Family

The humanistic assault on the family largely has been successful.[2] Too few Christian parents have implemented basic biblical principles for family living; fewer still recognize the principles applicable to the family that may be drawn from the Great Commission. In the midst of a pervasively humanistic culture, Christians have tended to live by the 1960s Greyhound Bus slogan: "Leave the driving to us." Too many children of believers become "prodigals" (Luke 15:11-13) by leaving the Church to seek the temporary comforts and pleasures our secular society affords. They have no awareness that the foundation of the technological progress that allows such creaturely comforts has been the Christian faith. They do not realize such luxury has lasted only due to the inertia of our past Christian heritage.[3]

Yet the Christian should with all seriousness view marriage as a covenantal institution with covenantal obligations. For marriage "is the primary training ground for the next generation. It is the primary institution for welfare, care of the young, care of the aged, and education. It is the primary agency of economic inheritance. *The family is therefore the primary institutional arrangement for fulfilling the terms of the dominion covenant* (Gen.

2. Phoebe Courtney, *The American Family Under Attack!* (Littleton, CO: Independent American, 1977; James Robison, *Attack on the Family* (Wheaton, IL: Tyndale, 1980); Charles Murray, *Losing Ground: American Social Policy 1950-1980* (New York: Basic Books, 1984). Even the federal government has recognized this, although it is not the least aware of the real nature of the problems; see: *White House Conference on Families: Listening to America's Families: Action for the 80's: The Report to the President, Congress and Families of the Nation* (Washington, D.C.: White House Conference on Families, October 1980).

3. For an insightful consideration of the effect of Scripture on economic and technological progress, see Gary North's *The Dominion Covenant: Genesis* (1982), *Moses and Pharaoh: Dominion Religion Versus Power Religion* (1985), and *The Sinai Strategy: Economics and the Ten Commandments* (1986). See also: David Chilton, *Productive Christians in an Age of Guilt Manipulators* (Tyler, TX: Institute for Christian Economics, 1981). For the role of Christianity in Western Culture, see: Francis Schaeffer, *How Should We Then Live? The Rise and Decline of Western Thought and Culture* (Old Tappan, NJ: Revell, 1976) and Hebert W. Schlossberg, *Idols for Destruction: Christian Faith and its Confrontation with American Society* (Nashville: Thomas Nelson, 1983).

1:26-28)."[4] In an important sense, as goes the family, so goes the faith; as goes the faith, so goes the culture.

Principles of the Covenantal Family

Although there are larger works on the family that should be consulted,[5] perhaps a listing of a few basics would prove helpful to those desirous to reclaim the family, bringing it under the sway of the Great Commission.

1. *Regular, content-oriented family devotions.* Primarily, these devotional times should impart sound biblical understanding and exhort our children to holiness in all of life. In addition, family devotions will provide a time of covenantal exercise, in order to enhance spiritual unity[6] in the family.[7] As DeMar so well puts it: "It must be made clear to all children that God is the head of the household. The father is a priest who conducts family worship services daily. The family must become God-centered in every way, including family ritual."[8]

Humanism is being imparted to our children as much by osmosis from our culture as by any other means. We and our children need the daily contact with the "living and active" Word of God to mold our thinking.[9] The Word of God imparts life and molds character (Psa. 19:7-14; 119:15-16). In the Great Commission Christ commands us to "teach all things" He taught us. We should begin this at a very early age with our children,[10] as covenantal baptism clearly obliges us.[11]

---

4. North, *Tools of Dominion*, pp. 214-215.

5. For example: Ray Sutton, *Who Owns the Family?* (Nashville: Thomas Nelson, 1986); Jay E. Adams, *Christian Living in the Home* (Phillipsburg, NJ: Presbyterian and Reformed, 1972); Wayne Mack, *Strengthening Your Marriage* (Phillipsburg, NJ: Presbyterian and Reformed, 1977).

6. Scripture is clear: the unity of the family ultimately depends on spiritual commitments. In fact, covenantal obligations override merely genetic relations. For example: Deut. 21:18-21; Matt. 10:34-39. See: Kenneth L. Gentry, Jr., "Thou Shalt Not Destroy the Family," *Journey*, Nov./Dec., 1986, pp. 19ff.

7. Psa. 1:2; 119:15-16, 23, 48, 78, 148.

8. Gary DeMar, *The Ruler of the Nations: Biblical Principles for Government* (Ft. Worth, TX: Dominion Press), p. 192. He has in this work and another of his, *God and Government: A Biblical and Historical Study* (Atlanta: American Vision, 1987), some excellent insights into the importance of "family government."

9. Psa. 119:130; Isa. 55:11; 1 Thess. 2:13; Heb. 4:12.

10. Psa. 71:17; Prov. 8:17; Eccl. 12:1; Matt. 19:13-14; 2 Tim. 3:14-15.

2. *Involved child rearing and discipline.* Our children expressly should be taught how to live the Christian life by the diligent application of biblical principles of child rearing[12] and discipline.[13] This is "discipling" in the home, as per the Great Commission (Matt. 28:19). This discipline should also include consistent church attendance, to worship Him who has "all authority in heaven and on earth" (Matt. 28:18).

The training of covenant children should not be left to others by parents too busy for their children. The regular "environmental"[14] influence of God's Word and Christ's gospel in daily family living is vital.[15] Children should be taught the legitimacy and practice of living under authority in society by witnessing it in the home through the headship of a loving, involved, and godly father.[16] Too often this duty has devolved almost wholly upon the mother, though she obviously has an important role, as well. Ultimately, biblical child discipline will work back to practical training in living under Christ's authority (Matt. 28:18).

Children also should be taught how to set goals for the long term (Matt. 28:20), rather than being allowed to drift about with the winds.

3. *Teaching the value of labor.* Apprenticeship of children in both family living and personal and corporate labor with a goal to self-sufficiency is important.

Ours is an intolerably irresponsible age. Christians must swim against the secular tide by instilling responsibility and diligence in their children.[17] The Christian is aware of the divinely ordained institution of labor from man's primordial

---

11. See Chapter 6 above.
12. Deut. 11:20-21; Josh. 24:15; Psalm 78:4-7; Prov. 4:1-4; 22:6; Eph. 6:4.
13. Prov. 19:18; 22:15; 23:13; 23:14; 29:15; 29:17; 13:24.
14. Regarding the ultimate personal environment in which we dwell, see: Psa. 139:7-12; Jer. 23:24; Acts 17:28. For a brief discussion of our "divine environment," see: Kenneth L. Gentry, Jr., *The Necessity of Christian Schooling* (Mauldin, SC: GoodBirth, 1985).
15. Gen. 18:19; Psa. 1:1-6; Deut. 6:5-25.
16. 1 Cor. 11:1ff; Eph. 5:22-6:4; Col. 3:20. See the insightful discussion in Gary North, *An Introduction to Christian Economics* (Nutley, NJ: Craig, 1973), ch. 21.
17. Prov. 12:24; 21:25; Rom. 12:11; 1 Tim. 5:8; 2 Thess. 3:10; Heb. 6:12.

beginning (Gen. 1:26-28; 2:15). The Commission is replete with verbal action. In addition to commands to disciple, baptize, and teach, one of its commands is *go*. This entails the notion of active labor.

The family involves the child's first experience with "culture" *(from which the word "nations" is derived*, Matt. 28:19). This is an aspect of that which the Great Commission sets before us by requiring our "discipling" (discipline). This obligates the believer to Christian labor. The family life should prepare the child for a life of labor for Christ in all of life.

4. *Teaching the value of money.* Training the child in Christian stewardship regarding both time (which is, in an important sense, money[18]) and resources should be a factor in Christian nurturing.

In a wealthy society children grow up thinking money grows on trees.[19] They should learn early the relationship between labor and the accruing of wealth. This should be done by assigning them productive chores in order to earn an allowance.[20] Many of Jesus' parables had to do with monetary matters,[21] and, thus, are directly involved in "teaching them to observe all that I commanded you" (Matt. 28:20).

In addition, children also should be encouraged both to save a portion of their money and to tithe on their increase to the church. Saving money forces them to operate with a view to the long term (which is a factor in the Great Commission, "I am with you always, even to the end," Matt. 28:20). The tithe demonstrates a bowing before the "all authority" of Christ (Matt. 28:18).

5. *Providing an inheritance.* An inheritance promises a reward for faithfulness, encourages a future orientation, and provides

---

18. North, *Dominion Covenant*, ch. 11; North, *Introduction to Christian Economics*, pp. 62ff.

19. Vaughn C. Nystrom, "A Ford is Not a Mango," in *The Freeman* (January, 1978), pp. 3-8.

20. Larry Burkett, *Using Your Money Wisely: Guidelines from Scripture* (Chicago: Moody, 1985), pp. 121ff.

21. For example, Matt. 13:44-46; 18:23-35; 20:1-16; 25:14-30; Luke 7:41-43; Luke 12-16-21; 15:8-32; 16:1-9; 16:19-31; 19:12-27.

a foundation from which to build for the next generation, thereby promoting progress by building on the fruits of the labors of others.[22]

Several of Christ's teachings had to do with inheritance.[23] The Bible obligates the provision of an inheritance for our offspring.[24] As in the Great Commission, we are to have a long view of history, not consuming all of our wealth for the moment. But ungodly children should be disinherited, "for the wealth of the sinner is laid up for the just."[25] Thus, we should be concerned to make plans that affect our children and children's children (Psa. 78:1-8) — they will be here for a long time.

6. *Formal Christian education.* Christian schooling should be encouraged and promoted vigorously by committed Christian parents, either through home schooling[26] or traditional classroom instruction.

The rampant secular humanism that permeates and dominates the government (public) school system is one of the very great strengths of humanism's influence.[27] Christians need to see that the thirty-plus hours a week their children spend in formal education in at least twelve years of their early development are undergirded and directed by Christian truth, rather than secular humanism.[28] The Great Commission demands

---

22. See discussion in Rousas John Rushdoony, *Institutes of Biblical Law* (Phillipsburg, NJ: Presbyterian & Reformed, 1973), 1:180ff. In volume 2 the following chapters are helpful: Chapters 2, 31-40.

23. Matt. 5:5; 19:29; 25:34; 21:38 Luke 12:13.

24. Prov. 13:22; 17:2; 19:4; Eccl. 7:11; 2 Cor. 12:13; 1 Tim. 5:8. See: Gary North, *The Sinai Strategy: Economics and the Ten Commandments* (Tyler, TX: Institute for Christian Economics, 1986), ch. 5 "Familistic Capital."

25. Prov. 13:22. See also the implications in: Prov. 17:2; Deut. 21:18-21; Matt. 7:6.

26. Mary Pride, *The Big Book of Home Learning* (Westchester, IL: Crossway, 1986).

27. Robert Thoburn, *The Children Trap: Biblical Principles for Education* (Nashville: Thomas Nelson, 1986); Phyllis Schlafly, ed., *Child Abuse in the Classroom* (Westchester, IL: Crossway, 1984); Mary Pride, *The Child Abuse Industry* (Westchester, IL: Crossway, 1986).

28. For a brief introduction to the Christian philosophy of education based on the Word of God, see: Gentry, *Christian Schooling* and Gentry, "Reformed Theology and Christian Education" in *Light for the World: Studies in the Reformed Thought* (Alberta, Edmonton: Still Waters Revival, forthcoming). For a fuller treatment, see: Cornelius Van Til, *Essays On Christian Education* (Nutley, NJ: Presbyterian and Reformed, 1971). R. J. Rushdoony, *The Philosophy of the Christian Curriculum* (Vallecito, CA: Ross House, 1981). R. J. Rushdoony, *Intellectual Schizophrenia: Culture, Crisis, and Education* (Nutley, NJ:

the "teaching of all things whatsoever" Christ teaches.

7. *Developing a home library and reading program.* Reading solid Christian literature (when it can be found) is an essential aspect of the mind-expanding exercise.

Elton Trueblood once commented, "It is the vocation of the Christian in every generation to out-think all opposition." Building a home library would make it easy for your own family to have access to good literature. It could also be made available for loaning out to others, thereby "teaching" others as Christ commanded us.

Of course, early in the child's reading program there should be frequent exposure to Scripture. The Word of God is unlike any other literature in that it is "living and powerful" (Heb. 4:12). It can and should be read at an early age, in that it makes one "wise unto salvation" (2 Tim. 3:14-15), becomes a part of the very character of the reader (Psa. 119:11), and equips one for "every good work" (2 Tim. 3:16-17).

8. *Neighborhood Bible studies on relevant issues.* The family should not withdraw within, but "go and make disciples" (Matt. 28:19).

An excellent means by which to promote Christian culture among families in your neighborhood is by setting up an informal, neighborly, family-oriented, and interesting study on matters of concern to your community.[29] In these studies, the gospel message and solution to the problems faced in every day life would be proffered in the context of friendly fellowship.

These types of Bible studies are academically helpful in getting God's truth before otherwise uninterested people. The average non-Christian gets his view of the world almost solely

---

Presbyterian and Reformed, 1961). For an excellent response to Christian excuses not to pursue Christian schooling, see: Lonn Oswalt, "Review of George Van Alstin's *The Christian and the Public Schools*, in Gary North, ed., *Christianity and Civilization* (Tyler, TX: Geneva Divinity School, 1983) 2:338-343.

29. For a fuller outline, see: Gary North, "Bread and Butter Neighborhood Evangelism" in *The Journal of Christian Reconstruction*, 7:2 (Winter, 1981) 114-140. For a helpful resource of topics, see: *Biblical Principles Concerning Issues of Importance to Godly Christians* (Plymouth, MA: Plymouth Rock Foundation, 1984). For a helpful introduction to Christian culture, see: Francis Nigel Lee, *The Central Significance of Culture* (Nutley, NJ: Presbyterian and Reformed, 1976).

through the secular humanist influenced media. To have an interesting and challenging study on relevant issues from a thought-provoking, distinctively Christian perspective may well influence those in attendance toward commitment to Christ. Such studies are also "environmentally" advantageous, giving the neighbor an inside look into and experience with a truly Christian home. The Christian home should be a model of true covenant living in both appearance and conduct. The Christian has something distinctively different to offer the world.

10

THE STATE AND
THE GREAT COMMISSION

And he carried me away in the Spirit to a great and high mountain, and showed me the great city, the holy Jerusalem, descending out of heaven from God. . . . And the nations of those who are saved shall walk in its light, and the kings of the earth bring their glory and honor into it (Revelation 21:10, 24).

As in the previous two chapters, I begin by referring again to the 1981 Association of Reformation Churches proposed addition to its confessional statement. Paragraph 5 of the document reads:

As a ministry of order, the mission of the state is to provide a peaceful environment in which the evangelical and cultural mandates may be carried out. Because of the sin of man, order and peace require the use of force, and thus to the state has been given the sword of justice. As the church implements Christ's work of redemption, so the state implements His work of vengeance. The terror of the sword has been given to man as the image and son of God, and thus the rule of justice must proceed in terms of the law of God revealed in the whole Scripture. To the extent that the revealed law of God is not implemented, the state does not fulfill its mission and becomes a tyranny. Only through the full application of Divine law can the widow, the orphan, the alien, and the poor be delivered form oppression; the family and the church be freed to perform their missions; and justice and right be established in all the world.[1]

Although it was not so designed by God, the State has become the dominant institution among men today. The temptation to Eve to "be like God" (Gen. 3:5) has been seized by heads of government throughout human history. Civil rulers have dared to seat themselves as gods (Isa. 14:4, 12-21; 2 Thess. 2:3-4; Rev. 13). With the State's monopoly of the sword (Rom. 13:1-4), this has brought untold woe upon man.

As I have shown in this book, the Christian worldview has wide-ranging implications, including for the State. Yet for much of this century (up until 1980), Christians have been content to sponsor "retreats," well away from civil issues — except for the misguided Christian influence in Prohibition.[2]

While maintaining a fundamental distinction between Church and State,[3] we still must recognize the Christian calling to affect all areas of life with the truth of Christ. The Great Commission is not without implications for civil government.[4]

1. *Concern for civil government.* Christians must have a concern for the function of the State as one of God's divinely ordained institutions.[5]

Christ calls us to "disciple all nations," and this reference to "nations" involves the idea of "cultures" (as per our earlier discussion). Consequently, we must have a concern for the governments of the nations, as an important aspect of culture.

---

1. "Of the Christian Mission" in *The Failure of the American Baptist Culture*, vol. 1 of *Christianity and Civilization* (Tyler, TX: Geneva Divinity School, 1982), p. 96.

2. For the biblical view of alcoholic beverage consumption (i.e., God allows its use in moderation and with circumspection), see: Kenneth L. Gentry, Jr., *The Christian and Alcoholic Beverages: A Biblical Perspective* (Grand Rapids: Baker, 1986).

3. See earlier statement at footnote 62 on p. 59, above. See also: Greg L. Bahnsen in Gary Scott Smith, ed., *God and Politics: Four Views on the Reformation of Civil Government* (Phillipsburg, NJ: Presbyterian and Reformed, 1989), pp. 21-53.

4. For more information in this area, see: Gary DeMar, *The Ruler of the Nations: Biblical Principles for Government* (Ft. Worth: Dominion, 1987). Greg L. Bahnsen, *House Divided: The Break-up of Dispensational Theology* (Tyler, TX: Institute for Christian Economics, 1989), Part I. Rus Walton, *One Nation Under God* (Old Tappen, NJ: Revell, 1975). Gary North, *Unconditional Surrender: God's Program for Victory* (Tyler, TX: Geneva Press, 1981). Ronald H. Nash, *Social Justice and the Christian Church* (Milford, MI: Mott Media, 1983). Rousas J. Rushdoony, *Politics of Guilt and Pity* (Fairfax, VA: Thoburn, 1978).

5. Rom. 13:1-3. Cp. Prov. 8:15-16; Jer. 27:5; Dan. 2:21; John 19:11; 1 Pet. 2:13-15.

To pietistically omit concern for civil government is to truncate the implications of the Great Commission.[6] We should note also that this retreatism would not be in accord with biblical precedent. Both Paul and Peter give express biblical principles applicable to civil government (Rom. 13:1-4[7]; 1 Pet. 2:13-17). John Baptist and Christ even rebuked civil authorities for their immoral conduct (Matt. 14:1-12; Mark 6:18; Luke 13:32). Scripture encourages our prayer for civil authority (Ezra 6:10; Psa. 72:1; Jer. 29:7).

2. *Obedience to civil government*. The various governmental spheres — family (1 Tim. 5:8; Eph. 5:22-6:4), Church (Heb. 13:17; 1 Pet. 5:1-5), and State (1 Tim. 2:2-3; 1 Pet. 2:14) are ordained by God for our good.

Paul and Peter specifically oblige us to submit to civil governmental authority (Rom. 13:2-7; 1 Pet. 2:12-17). Since the Great Commission shows Christ laying claim to "all authority" on earth, civil government must submit to His design. As a basic and general rule, therefore, the Christian should live an orderly, Christ exhibiting life in terms of his civil relations (1 Pet. 2:15).

Nevertheless, the Christian at all times holds God and Christ as supreme authority and must refuse any governmental directive which would obligate his doing that which is contrary to God's revealed will.[8] The government may not act as God;[9] it

---

6. The retreat of fundamentalists from politics for most of this century is well known. It was generally due to an unstudied lack due to theological superficiality, rather than to a researched conviction. Recently, however, there has been a resurgence of well-thought out (though ill-conceived) anabaptist thought, calling for Christians to resist seeking political influence. See: Charles Scriven, "The Reformation Radicals Ride Again" and Stanley Hauerwas and William H. Sillimon, "Peculiar People" in *Christianity Today* (March 5, 1990), pp. 13ff.

7. Paul's statements here are ideals for government, not an historical account of Roman government.

8. For more information see: Junius Brutus, *A Defence of Liberty Against Tyrants* (Edmonton, Alberta: Still Waters Revival Books, 1989 [rep. 1689]). Herbert Schlossberg, *Idols for Destruction: Christian Faith and Its Confrontation with American Society* (Nashville: Thomas Nelson, 1983). Francis Schaeffer, *A Christian Manifesto* (Westchester, IL: Crossway, 1981, chs. 7-10. Gary North, *The Dominion Covenant: Genesis* (Tyler, TX: Institute for Christian Economics, 1982), ch. 19. Gary North, ed., *Christianity and Civilization* (Tyler, TX: Geneva Divinity School, 1983), vol 2: "The Theology of Christian Resistance" and vol. 3: "Tactics of Christian Resistance."

9. Matt. 22:21; Acts 12:20-23. Cp. Isaiah's taunt against the king of Babylon, Isa.

does not possess unimpeachable authority.[10] Only Christ has "all authority" to command us (Matt. 28:18).

3. *Exposing evil governmental policies.* In that man is sinful, government easily lapses into sin and must be exposed for its wickedness.

Unrighteousness anywhere is hated by God. In the sphere of civil government wickedness especially has horrible and dangerous consequences. Bowing to the ultimate authority of Christ (Matt. 28:18) and seeking actively to "disciple the nations" (Matt. 28:19), the Christian will "expose the works of darkness" (Eph. 5:11).[11] He will be recognized as one at odds with certain governmental policies because of his commitment to Christ (Acts 5:21, 29; 17:7-10).

4. *Involvement in civil government.* In that faith must be exhibited in works (Jms. 2:14-26), and prayer must be undergirded by labor,[12] we should engage ourselves actively in our governmental process, and not just "be concerned."

The call to "disciple the nations" involves actively and diligently setting forth the claims of Christ even before governments. The Christian should promote governmental polices rooted in God's Law.[13] One of the express purposes for God's establishment of Israel under His Law was that it give an example to the governments of the world regarding righteous law.[14] Civil governments are to glorify God in governing their populations[15] by founding their governments on God's Law.

In doing this, we should recognize the importance of local governmental offices, because: (a) Most higher, federal offices have been gained by those experienced in lower, more local governments. Thus, in the long run (Matt. 28:20), this will reap

---

14:4, 12-21.

10. Exo. 1:15-20; Josh. 2; Dan. 3:8-30; Acts 5:29.

11. For help in this area, see: William Billings, *The Christian's Political Action Manual* (Washington, D.C.: National Christian Action Council, 1980).

12. Cp. Matt. 6:11 with 2 Thess. 3:10.

13. Psa. 119:46; 148:11,13; 1 Tim. 1:8-10; Rom. 13:4-9. See Greg L. Bahnsen, *By This Standard* (Tyler, TX: Institute for Christian Economics, 1985) and Rushdoony, *Institutes of Biblical Law*, 2 vols.

14. Deut. 4:5-8; Isa. 24:5; 51:4; Psa. 2:9-10; 119:118.

15. 2 Sam. 23:3; 2 Chron. 19;6-7; Psa. 2:10-12; 148:1, 11.

rewards. (b) We have more influence on local government than on federal government. (c) It costs less, thereby encouraging stewardship.

5. *Promotion of Christian distinctives in government.* In that Christ has "all authority," we should labor in *the long term* for a recognition of and submission to Christ's authority (not the Church's!) in the United States Constitution.

Although any present discussion of reverent submission to Christ in governmental affairs might seem contrary to the "American Way," it has not always been so. The earliest colonial charters and state constitutions — even into the 1800s — were distinctly Christian covenants, fully recognizing Christ's "authority on earth" (Matt. 28:18). It has been through the decline of a full-orbed Christian "discipling" program and biblical witness (Matt. 28:19) that we have ended up with a secular state. This decline is largely traceable back to the negative influence of the Great Awakening in the 1700s.[16]

Christians need to begin rethinking their understanding of governmental authority. "He that ruleth over men must be just, ruling in the fear of God" (2 Sam. 23:3). In the long run, due to the predestined expansion of Christ's kingdom, all kings and nations will bow to Christ.[17] And since God normally works through means, we need to realize that the intellectual preparations should be begun now in anticipation of a cultural paradigm shift. All of this will involve registering to vote, voting, precinct work, running for office, and other such endeavors.

---

16. Gary North, *Political Polytheism: The Myth of Pluralism* (Tyler, TX: Institute for Christian Economics, 1989).

17. "And, with reference to the times of the New Testament, when 'the abundance of the sea shall be converted, and their forces come unto' [the Church], he hath promised, that 'kings shall be her nursing fathers; — her officers peace, and her exactors righteousness.' This is connected with the "advancement of the interests of the meditorial [*sic*] kingdom of our Lord Jesus Christ, which is *in*, but not *of* this world, and *as* subservient to which the kingdom of providence is committed unto him."' Thomas M'Crie, *Statement of the Difference Between the Profession of the Reformed Church of Scotland, as Adopted by Seceders, and the Profession Contained in the New Testimony and Other Acts, Lately Adopted by the General Associate Synod; etc.* (Edmunton, AL: Still Waters Revival, forthcoming [1807; 1871]), p. 133

Conclusion

The Great Commission has important, direct bearings on the three foundational societal institutions, the family, the Church, and the State. The full-orbed character of the Great Commission demonstrates both its greatness and its practicality to life. The eyes of the Lord are in every place beholding the evil and the good (Prov. 15:3), not just in the heart, but in all areas of life.

If Christians are to preserve the very greatness of the Great Commission, they need to see its applicability to all of life. To do so will require a radical re-orientation in our thinking, a biblical re-orientation. We need to reclaim the Pauline spirit:

Therefore I testify to you this day that I am innocent of the blood of all men. For I have not shunned to declare to you the whole counsel of God. Therefore take heed to yourselves and to all the flock, among which the Holy Spirit has made you overseers, to shepherd the church of God which He purchased with His own blood (Acts 20:26-28).

Part IV

IMPLICATIONS

11

MILLENNIAL ORIENTATION AND THE GREAT COMMISSION

For He must reign till He has put all enemies under His feet. The last enemy that will be destroyed is death. For He has put all things under His feet. . . . Therefore, my beloved brethren, be steadfast, immovable, always abounding in the work of the Lord, knowing that your labor is not in vain in the Lord (1 Corinthians 15:25-27a, 58).

"Eschatology" is that field of study in theology that is concerned with "the last things."[1] As I have shown in various places in the preceding chapters, eschatology has a tremendous effect on the Christian's worldview and, consequently, on his practical, daily living. Eschatological systems are generally categorized in regard to their approach to the "millennium."[2] The idea of the millennium is derived from Revelation 20:1-6, where the designation of a "one thousand" year reign of Christ is treated (though *only* in these six verses!).

Comparative Summary of Millennial Views

The Great Commission is greatly affected by our understanding of eschatology. Ironically, there is one eschatological position that cites the Great Commission as evidence of its biblical warrant: postmillennialism. This is the viewpoint pre-

---

1   "Eschatology" is derived from the Greek. *eschatos*, i.e. "last," and *logos*, i.e "word."
2   "Millennium" is derived from the Latin *mille*, i.e "thousand," and *annum*, i.e "year"

sented in this book. In that the Great Commission is so affected by one's eschatological system, it might be helpful to provide a brief summary of several of the leading features of the four major evangelical eschatological systems.[3] It should be understood that any particular adherent to one of the following views may disagree with some aspect as I have presented it. There are always differences of nuance among adherents to any particular system. Nevertheless, the presentation attempts to portray accurately the general, leading features of the systems. The systems will be presented in alphabetical order.

Amillennialism

Definition: That view of prophecy that expects no wide-ranging, long-lasting earthly manifestation of kingdom power until Christ returns, other than in the salvation of the elect. Amillennialist Kuiper writes: "'The thousand years' of Revelation 20 represent in symbolic language a long and complete period; namely, the period of history from Christ's ascension into heaven until his second coming. Throughout that age Christ reigns and the saints in glory reign with him (vs. 4). Satan is bound in the sense of not being permitted to lead the pagan nations against Christendom (vss. 2-3) . . . . During that period also takes place under the rule of Christ what may be termed the parallel development of the kingdom of light and that of darkness . . . . Toward the end of 'the thousand years' Satan will be loosed for a little while. Those will be dark days for the church of God . . . . Christ will return in ineffable glory and, having raised the dead, will sit in judgment on all men (Rev. 20:12,13)."[4]

Descriptive Features: 1. The Church Age is the kingdom era prophesied by the Old Testament prophets.[5] Israel and the Church are merged into one body in Christ to form the Israel

---

3. For more detailed information, see: Robert G. Clouse, ed., *The Meaning of the Millennium: Four Views* (Downer's Grove, IL: Inter-Varsity Press, 1977).

4. R. B. Kuiper, *God-Centered Evangelism* (Grand Rapids: Baker, 1961), pp. 208-209.

5. Amillennialist Anthony Hoekema sees the fulfillment of the kingdom prophecies in the New Heavens and New Earth, rather than in the Church. Anthony Hoekema, *The Bible and the Future* (Grand Rapids: Wm. B. Eerdmans, 1979). See my footnote 2, p. 147

of God.

2. Satan is bound during His earthly ministry at Christ's First Coming. Satan is progressively restricted by the proclamation of the gospel.

3. Christ rules in the hearts of believers. There will be but occasional, short-lived influences of Christianity on culture, although the Christian should, nevertheless, labor toward a Christian culture. Hence: the system is amillennial (no-millennium), in that there is no visible, earthly manifestation of millennial conditions as in the pre- and postmillennial systems. The "thousand years" is held to be a symbolic figure representative of a vast expanse of time.

4. History will gradually worsen as the growth of evil accelerates toward the end. This will culminate in the Great Tribulation.

5. Christ will return to end history, resurrect and judge all men, and establish the eternal order.

Representative Adherents: In the ancient church: Hermas (first century) and Augustine (A.D. 354-430). In the modern church: Jay E. Adams, Hendrikus Berkhof, Louis Berkhof, Theodore Graebner, W. J. Grier, Floyd E. Hamilton, William Hendriksen, J. W. Hodges, Anthony Hoekema, Abraham Kuyper, Philip Mauro, George Murray, Albertus Pieters, and Geerhardus Vos (possibly).

Dispensational Premillennialism

Definition: A theological system, arising around 1830, that understands the Scripture to teach that God has two separate programs for two distinct peoples: national Israel and the Church. Since Pentecost the program for the Church has been in operation. The Church will continue to operate as a spiritual witness to the nations until God secretly raptures Christians out of the world. Soon thereafter Christ will return to the earth to set up an earthly kingdom of one thousand years duration.[6]

Descriptive Features: 1. The Church Age is a wholly unforseen

---

6. See: H. Wayne House and Thomas D. Ice, *Dominion Theology: Blessing Or Curse?* (Portland, OR: Multnomah, 1988), pp. 418-420, 422.

mystery, which was altogether unknown to and unexpected by the Old Testament prophets.

2. God has a separate and distinct program and plan for racial Israel, as distinguished from the Church. The Church of Jesus Christ is a parenthetical aside in the original plan of God.

3. The Kingdom offered by Christ in the first century was postponed until the future.

4. The Church experiences some small scale successes in history, but ultimately loses influence, fails in her mission, is corrupted as worldwide evil increases and intensifies toward the end of the Church Age.

5. Christ returns secretly in the sky to rapture living saints and to resurrect the bodies of deceased saints (the first resurrection). These are removed out of the world before the Great Tribulation. The judgment of the saints is accomplished in heaven during the seven year period before Christ's return to the earth.

6. At the conclusion of the seven year Great Tribulation, Christ returns to the earth with His glorified saints in order to establish and personally administer a Jewish political kingdom headquartered at Jerusalem for 1000 years. During this time Satan is bound and the temple and sacrificial system is re-established in Jerusalem as memorials. Hence: the system is *"premillennial,"* in that Christ returns *prior* to the millennium, which is a literal 1000 years.

7. Toward the end of the Millennial Kingdom, Satan is loosed and Christ is surrounded and attacked at Jerusalem.

8. Christ calls down fire from heaven to destroy His enemies. The resurrection (the second resurrection) and judgment of the wicked occurs. The eternal order begins.

Representative Adherents: In the ancient church: None (created *ca.* 1830). In the modern church: Donald G. Barnhouse, W. E. Blackstone, James M. Brookes, L. S. Chafer, John Nelson Darby, Charles Lee Feinberg, A. C. Gaebelein, Norman Geisler, Harry Ironside, Hal Lindsey, C. H. MacIntosh, G. Campbell Morgan, J. Dwight Pentecost, Charles C. Ryrie, C. I Scofield, John F. Walvoord, and Warren Wiersbe.

Historic Premillennialism

Definition: That ancient view of prophecy that sees the present age as one in which the Church will expand, but with little influence in the world, other than calling out the elect to salvation. At the end of this age the Lord will return and resurrect believers and will establish His kingdom over the earth for 1000 years. At the end of that period will occur the resurrection of the wicked. Premillennialist Ladd writes: "the gospel is not to conquer the world and subdue all nations to itself. Hatred, conflict, and war will continue to characterize the age until the coming of the Son of Man" and "evil will mark the course of the age."[7]

Descriptive Features: 1. The New Testament era Church is the *initial* phase of Christ's kingdom as prophesied by the Old Testament prophets.

2. The New Testament Church will win many victories, but ultimately will fail in its mission, lose influence, and become corrupted as worldwide evil increases toward the end of the Church Age.

3. The Church will pass through a future, worldwide, unprecedented time of travail, known as the Great Tribulation, which will punctuate the end of contemporary history.

4. Christ will return at the end of the Tribulation to rapture the Church, resurrect deceased saints, and conduct the judgment of the righteous in the "twinkling of an eye."

5. Christ then will descend to the earth with His glorified saints, fight the battle of Armageddon, bind Satan, and establish a worldwide, political kingdom, which will be personally administered by Him for 1000 years from Jerusalem. Hence, the designation "premillennial, in that Christ returns prior to the millennium, which is understood as a literal 1000 years.

6. At the end of the millennial reign, Satan will be loosed and a massive rebellion against the kingdom and a fierce assault against Christ and His saints will occur.

7. God will intervene with fiery judgment to rescue Christ

---

7. George Eldon Ladd, *Theology of the New Testament* (Grand Rapids: Wm. B. Eerdmans, 1974), pp. 202, 203.

and the saints. The resurrection and the judgment of the wicked will occur and the eternal order will begin.

Representative Adherents: In the Ancient church: Papias (A.D. 60-130) and Justin Martyr (A.D. 100-165). In the modern church: Henry Alford, E. B. Elliott, A. R. Faussett, Henry W. Frost, H. G. Guinness, Robert H. Gundry, S. H. Kellog, George Eldon Ladd, Alexander Reese, and Nathaniel West.

Postmillennialism

Definition: Postmillennialism is that system of eschatology which understands the Messianic kingdom to have been founded upon the earth during the earthly ministry and through the redemptive labors of the Lord Jesus Christ in fulfillment of Old Testament prophetic expectation. The nature of that kingdom is essentially redemptive and spiritual and will exercise a transformational socio-cultural influence in history, as more and more people are converted to Christ. Postmillennialism confidently anticipates a time in earth history in which the gospel will have won the victory throughout the earth in fulfillment of the Great Commission. After an extended period of gospel prosperity, earth history will be drawn to a close by the personal, visible, bodily return of Jesus Christ (accompanied by a literal resurrection and a general judgment).

Descriptive Features: 1. The Church is the kingdom prophesied in the Old Testament era and is the millennial age. It is composed of Jew and Gentile merged into one body in Christ, as the New Israel of God.

2. The kingdom was established in its mustard seed form by Christ during His earthly ministry at His First Coming. It will develop gradualistically through time.[8]

3. Satan was bound by Christ in His earthly ministry and is progressively hindered as the gospel spreads.

---

8. It does not develop uniformly, but gradualistically in spurts. In a sense, it is like seed, which is planted and grows and produces other seed (see: Matt. 13:3-9, 23). Thus, we can expect it to grow in certain areas and perhaps even to die, but eventually to come back, because the productivity of seed involves its death and renewal (see: John 12:24; 1 Cor. 15:36). In addition, we may expect God's pruning from time to time (John 15:5-6).

4. The Great Tribulation occurred in the first century at the destruction of the Jewish Temple and Jerusalem, because of Israel's rejection of their Messiah, Jesus Christ.

5. The kingdom will grow and develop until eventually it exercises a dominant and universal gracious influence in a long era of righteousness, peace, and prosperity on the earth and in history.

6. Toward the end of Christ's spiritual millennial reign, Satan will be loosed and a brief rebellion by the remaining minority, unconverted sinners against Christianity will occur.

7. Christ will return *after* the millennium to avenge Himself upon the ungrateful rebells and to resurrect and judge all men. He will then usher in the eternal order. Hence: the system is *post*millennial, in that Christ returns after the millennium, although the "1000 years" is held to be a symbolic figure representative of a vast expanse of time.

Representative Adherents: In the ancient church: Eusebius (A.D. 260-340) and Athanasius (A.D. 296-372). In the modern church: (traditional) J. A. Alexander, O. T. Allis, David Brown, Lorraine Boettner, John Calvin, Roderick Campbell, David Chilton, John Jefferson Davis, Jonathan Edwards, A. A. and Charles A. Hodge, Erroll Hulse, Marcellus Kik, John Murray, B. B. Warfield; (covenantal or theonomic) Greg Bahnsen, Francis Nigel Lee, Gary North, R. J. Rushdoony — and the Westminster Confession of Faith and many of the Puritans.

The Biblical and Theological Superiority of Postmillennialism

There are two sets of primary considerations: biblical and theological. The former relates to the actual biblical texts; the latter relates to the implications of these texts.

Biblical Considerations

1. Contrary to dispensationalism's view of the Church Age being unforeseen by the prophets of the Old Testament, see: Acts 2:16-17; 3:24-26; 15:14-18; Galatians 3:8.

2. Contrary to dispensationalism's view that the kingdom

promises refer to national Israel rather than to the Church as the New Israel of God, see: Galatians 3:28-19; 6:16; Ephesians 2:12-22; Philippians 3:3; Romans 2:28-29; and 1 Peter 2:5-9.

3. Contrary to dispensationalism, Christ did establish His kingdom in the first century, see: Mark 1:15; 9:1; Luke 11:20; 17:20-21; John 18:33-37; Colossians 1:13.

4. Contrary to dispensationalism, Christ is now enthroned and ruling over His kingdom, see: Acts 2:29-35; Romans 8:34; Hebrews 1:3; 10:12-13; Revelation 1:5-6; 3:21.

5. Contrary to dispensationalism and historic premillennialism, Christ's kingdom is not an earthly-political kingdom[9], but a spiritual-redemptive kingdom, see: Luke 17:20-21; Romans 14:17; John 18:36-37.

6. Contrary to dispensationalism and historic premillennialism, Satan was bound in the first century, see: Matthew 12:28-29; Luke 10:18; John 12:31; Colossians 2:15; Hebrews 2:14; 1 John 3:8.

7. Contrary to dispensationalism, historic premillennialism, and amillennialism, the Great Tribulation occurred in the first century (at the destruction of the temple and Jerusalem), see: Matthew 24:34 (cp. Matt. 24:2, 3, 15, 21); Revelation 1:1, 3, 9; 3:10 (cp. Revelation 7:14).

8. Contrary to dispensationalism, historic premillennialism, and amillennialism, the Church will not fail in its task of evangelizing the world, see: Matthew 13:31-32; 16:18; 28:18-20.

9. Contrary to dispensationalism, historic premillennialism, and amillennialism, Christ's redemptive labors will hold a universal sway in the world before the end of contemporary history, see: Matthew 13:31-32; John 1:29; 3:17; 4:42; 12:31-32; 1 Corinthians 15:20-26; 2 Corinthians 5:17-21; Hebrews 1:3, 13; 10:12-13.

10. Contrary to dispensationalism and historic premillennialism, there is but one resurrection and one judgment, which occur simultaneously at the end of history, see: Daniel 12:2; Matthew 24:31-32; John 5:28-29; 6:39-40; 11:40; Acts 24:15.

11. Contrary to dispensationalism and historic premillen-

---

9. Although Christ's kingdom *does* have an earthly-political influence.

nialism, when Christ comes, history will end, see: 1 Corinthians 15:20-25; Matthew 13:29-30; 1 Thessalonians 4:13-17.

Theological Considerations

1. In distinction to dispensationalism, historic premillennialism, and amillennialism, postmillennialism is optimistic in its historical outlook, see: Psalm 2; 72; Isaiah 2:1-4; 9:6-7; 11:1-9; Matthew 28:18-20.

2. In distinction to dispensationalism and historic premillennialism, postmillennialism does not allow for a monstrous and absurd mixing of immortal, gloried and resurrected saints with mortal, unglorified men upon the earth for a 1000 year period of interaction.

3. In distinction to dispensationalism and historic premillennialism, in postmillennialism Christ will not undergo a "second humiliation" on earth (or ever).

4. Contrary to dispensationalism, postmillennialism does not teach there is coming a return to "weak and beggarly elements," such as the temple, sacrifices, Jewish exaltation, and such, see: Galatians 4:9; Hebrews 9-10; 1 Peter 2:5-9; Ephesians 2:20-21; 1 Corinthians 3:16; 6:19; 2 Corinthians 6:16ff.

The Great Commission and Dispensationalism

It is alarming that some among dispensationalists view the Great Commission as a *Jewish mandate not incumbent upon the Church in this age!* Let us cite just a few brief quotations in demonstration of this remarkable distortion of biblical theology.

E. W. Bullinger (19th century), well known for his *Companion Bible*, states very clearly of Matthew 28:18-20: "this particular commission was . . . postponed."[10] Here the Postponed Kingdom Theory of dispensationalism is tied into the disavowal of the contemporary obligation to promote the Great Commission.

Arno C. Gaebelein (d. 1945) wrote of the Great Commission in his popular *Annotated Bible*: "This is the *Kingdom* Commission

---

10. E. W. Bullinger, *The Companion Bible* (London: Samuel Bagster and Sons, rep. 1970 [n.d.]) p. 1380.

. . . . A time is coming when this great commission here will be carried out by a remnant of Jewish disciples . . . ."[11] In keeping with the Postponed Kingdom Theory, Gaebelein also puts the Commission's institution off into the future.

A more recent dispensationalist, Charles F. Baker, explains that when the Great Commission was given "there had been no revelation as yet that the program of the prophesied Kingdom was to be interrupted by this present dispensation of the mystery."[12] George Williams agrees.[13] (Notice should be made of the fact that the Church Age "interrupted" God's Kingdom Program.)

Dispensationalist Stanley Toussaint, in his recent commentary on Matthew, mentions the debate among current dispensationalists,[14] while another dispensationalist David L. Turner comments regarding modern dispensationalists that "*most* would agree that the stirring mandate for discipleship with which Matthew concludes is incumbent upon the Church today."[15]

Conclusion

The study of eschatology is an important matter for the Christian. What we believe the future holds for us and our children has a great impact on the prioritizing of our life's concerns. Eschatology should not be approached as if but an interesting aside to the study of Scripture. It is a fundamental aspect of it, having a great bearing even on the understanding of evangelism itself.

In closing, I would like to point out to the reader that I write a monthly newsletter that analyzes the numerous distortions inherent in dispensationalism. Despite its widespread

11. Arno C. Gaebelein, *The Annotated Bible*, vol. 6: *Matthew to the Acts* (Traveler's Rest, SC: Southern Bible Book House, n.d.), p. 61.
12. Charles F. Baker, *A Dispensational Theology* (Grand Rapids: Grace Bible College, 1971), p. 558.
13. George Williams, *The Student's Commentary on the Holy Scriptures* (4th ed.: Grand Rapids: Kregal, 1949), pp. 730-731.
14. Stanley D. Toussaint, *Behold the King!* (Portland, OR: Multnomah, 1980), p. 318.
15. David L. Turner, "The Structure and Sequence of Matthew 24:1-41: Interaction with Evangelical Treatments," *Grace Theological Journal* 10:1 (Spring, 1989) 6 (emphasis mine).

popularity, dispensationalism has brought a number of severe aberrations into biblical theology. The reader can receive a free six month subscription to the newsletter by writing to the following address:

Dispensationalism in Transition
Institute for Christian Economics
P. O. Box 8000
Tyler, Texas 75711

12

PESSIMISM AND
THE GREAT COMMISSION

Then Caleb quieted the people before Moses, and said, "Let us go up at once and take possession, for we are well able to overcome it." But the men who had gone up with him said, "We are not able to go up against the people, for they are stronger than we." And they gave the children of Israel a bad report of the land which they had spied out, saying, "The land through which we have gone as spies is a land that devours its inhabitants, and all the people whom we saw in it are men of great stature. There we saw the giants (the descendants of Anak came from the giants); and we were like grasshoppers in our own sight, and so we were in their sight." Then all the congregation lifted up their voices and cried, and the people wept that night" (Numbers 13:30-14:1).

For whatever is born of God overcomes the world. And this is the victory that has overcome the world; our faith (1 John 5:4).

The Issue

The dispensationalist Christian has a different understanding of the Great Commission from the postmillennialist. In addition, so do many amillennialists and historic (non-dispensational) premillennialists. And that difference of understanding is not merely one of a shading of grey tones, but of a stark contrast of black and white, as we shall see.

The three eschatological systems mentioned in the preceding paragraph may be categorized as "pessimistic," whereas the postmillennial view may be seen as "optimistic." In categorizing them as "pessimistic," I am speaking of the following issues:

(1) As systems of gospel proclamation each teaches the gospel of Christ will not exercise any majority influence in the world before Christ's return;

(2) As systems of historical understanding each, in fact, holds the Bible teaches there are prophetically determined, irresistible trends downward toward chaos in the outworking and development of history; and therefore

(3) As systems for the promotion of Christian discipleship each dissuades the Church from anticipating and laboring for wide-scale success in influencing the world for Christ during this age.

The pessimism/optimism question has very much to do with the *practical* endeavors of Christians in the world *today*. All evangelical Christians are optimistic in the *ultimate* sense that God will miraculously win the war against sin and Satan at the end of history by direct, supernatural intervention, either in a pre-millennial kingdom introduced by the Second Coming[1] or at the final judgment, which introduces the New Heavens and New Earth.[2]

A recent illustration of the practical effects of a pessimistic worldview is found in a statement recorded by Charles Colson. He speaks of Christians ceasing to attempt to be an influence for righteousness in the political and social arena: A "prominent evangelical, veteran of the battles of the eighties, told me he was through. 'Why bother?' he confided privately."[3]

---

1. For example: "The Bible expects the world to be conquered not by Christianity, but only by the second coming of Christ." John F. Walvoord, "Review of House Divided. By Greg L. Bahnsen and Kenneth L. Gentry, Jr." in *Bibliotheca Sacra* (July-September, 1990), p. 372. "The premillennialist sees Christ intervening catastrophically in a moment of history, resulting in an establishment of his mediatorial rule." H. Wayne House and Thomas D. Ice, *Dominion Theology: Blessing or Curse?* (Portland, OR: Multnomah, 1988), p. 140.
2. "Old Testament prophecies interpreted by postmillennialists as referring to a future millennial golden age picture the final state of the redeemed community. . . [in] a new heaven and a new earth." Anthony Hoekema, *The Bible and the Future* (Grand Rapids: Wm. B. Eerdmans, 1979), p. 177.
3. Charles Colson, "From a Moral Majority to a Persecuted Minority," *Christianity*

148   THE GREATNESS OF THE GREAT COMMISSION

Examples of Eschatological Pessimism

Two best-selling authors in our day, well-known representatives of dispensationalism, are Hal Lindsey[4] and Dave Hunt.[5] These men have recognized the significant difference between their dispensational understanding of the Great Commission and its implications and the postmillennial understanding with its implications. In fact, they have written recent works for the very purpose of countering the postmillennial understanding of the Great Commission.[6] But, as we shall see, these two men are not the only evangelicals who dispute the historic postmillennial view.

Dispensationalism

The dispensational view sees the Great Commission in this age as having only a very restricted influence in bringing men to salvation. The hundreds of thousands of evangelical Christians who read dispensational literature have had continually drummed into their minds the teaching that under no circumstance will the gospel be victorious in our age. Let me demonstrate this by a quick survey of quotations from several dispensational authors.

Hal Lindsey states the situation about as strongly as can be: "Christ died for us in order to rescue us from this present evil age. [Titus 2:11-15] show what our focus, motivation, and hope should be in this present age. We are to live with the constant expectation of the any-moment appearing of our LORD to this earth."[7]

H. A. Ironside notes in his comments on the Great Commission: "We know that not all nations will accept the message in

---

Today 34:8 (May 14, 1990) 80.

4. Lindsey is best known for his multi-million best-seller, *The Late Great Planet Earth* (1970).

5. Hunt is best known for his best-seller, *The Seduction of Christianity: Spiritual Discernment in the Last Days* (Eugene, OR: Harvest House, 1985).

6. Hal Lindsey, *The Road to Holocaust* (New York: Bantam, 1989). Dave Hunt, *Whatever Happened to Heaven?* (Eugene, OR: Harvest House, 1988).

7 Lindsey, *Holocaust*, p. 279.

this age of grace."[8] William MacDonald points out that the Great Commission "does not presuppose world conversion."[9] In fact, the opposite is true, according to J. Dwight Pentecost, for "during the course of the age there will be a decreasing response to the sowing of the seed" of the Gospel.[10] Stanley Toussaint concurs, when he notes that "evil will run its course and dominate the [Church] age."[11] Warren Wiersbe agrees: "Some make this parable [of the Mustard Seed] teach the worldwide success of the Gospel. But that would contradict what Jesus taught in the first parable. If anything, the New Testament teaches a growing decline in the ministry of the Gospel as the end of the age draws near."[12] In fact, he notes later that "it would seem that Satan is winning! But the test is at *the end* of the age, not *during* the age."[13]

Charles C. Ryrie denies any postmillennial hope based on the Great Commission, when he speaks in opposition to the postmillennial hope: "Their confidence in the power of God causes them to believe that the Great Commission will be fulfilled in that most of the world will be saved."[14] The postmillennial view of Church history is wrong, he says, because "defection and apostasy, among other things, will characterize that entire period."[15] Consequently, Dave Hunt argues that "only a small percentage of mankind is willing . . . to come to Christ in repentance and be born again by the Spirit of God" and that "the vast majority of people will continue to reject Christ in the future just as they have in the past."[16] Hal Lindsey scorns the

---

8. Harry A. Ironside, *Expository Notes on the Gospel of Matthew* (New York: Loizeaux Bros., 1948), p. 405.

9. William MacDonald, *The Gospel of Matthew: Behold Your King* (Kansas City: Walterick, 1974), p. 323.

10. J. Dwight Pentecost, *Things to Come: A Study in Biblical Eschatology* (Grand Rapids: Zondervan, 1957), p. 146.

11. Stanley D. Toussaint, *Behold the King* (Portland, OR: Multnomah, 1980), p. 182.

12. Warren W. Wiersbe, *Bible Expositor's Commentary*, 2 vols., (Wheaton, IL: Victor, 1989), 1:46.

13. *Ibid.*

14. Charles C. Ryrie, *Basic Theology* (Wheaton, IL: Victor, 1986), pp. 441-442.

15. *Ibid.*, p. 461.

16. Dave Hunt, *Whatever Happened to Heaven?* (Eugene, OR: Harvest House, 1988), p. 178.

postmillennialist for believing "that virtually the whole world population will be converted. I wish this were possible, but God Himself says that it is not."[17] In fact, "the world will progressively harden its heart against the Gospel and plunge itself into destruction."[18]

Historic Premillennialism

Historic premillennialists would concur with such a dismal prospect for the widespread success of the gospel. J. Barton Payne believes that "evil is present in our world as predicted in the Holy Books" (of the Bible). This evil must occur because it is a forecast of Christ's soon return.[19] Robert H. Mounce laments that "it is difficult to see from history alone any cause for optimism." He is certain that it will be a "persecuted church [that] will witness the victorious return of Christ,"[20] rather than a world-conquering church. George Eldon Ladd concurs: "In spite of the fact that God had invaded history in Christ, and in spite of the fact that it was to be the mission of Jesus' disciples to evangelize the entire world (Matt. 24:!4), the world would remain an evil place. False christs would arise who would lead many astray. Wars, strife, and persecution would continue. Wickedness would abound so as to chill the love of many."[21]

Amillennialism

Among amillennialists we discover the same sort of despair. Cornelius Vanderwaal writes that "I do not believe in inevitable progress toward a much better world in this dispensation" and God's "church has no right to take an optimistic, triumphalistic attitude."[22] H. de Jongste and J. M. van Krimpen are forth-

---

17. Lindsey, *Holocaust*, p. 49.
18. *Ibid.*, p. 36.
19. J. Barton Payne, *Biblical Prophecy for Today* (Grand Rapids: Baker, 1978), p. 10.
20. Robert H. Mounce, *The Book of Revelation* (*New International Commentary on the New Testament*) (Grand Rapids: Wm. B. Eerdmans, 1977), pp. 44, 47.
21. George Eldon Ladd, *The Last Things: An Eschatology for Laymen* (Grand Rapids: Wm. B. Eerdmans, 1978), p. 58.
22. Cornelius Vanderwaal, *Hal Lindsey and Biblical Prophecy* (St. Catherine's, Ontario: Paideia, 1978), pp. 44, 45.

right in their declaration that "there is no room for optimism: towards the end, in the camps of the satanic and the anti-Christ, culture will sicken, and the Church will yearn to be delivered from its distress."[23] Amillennialist Donald Guthrie, according to dispensationalist John F. Walvoord, "readily agrees that the biblical point of view is pessimistic, that is, the world as it is now constituted will not be revived and improved, but instead, will be destroyed and replaced."[24]

Christian Cultural Models

At this juncture we should recall our opening questions from our introduction: (1) What is the Great Commission? (2) What is the goal of the Great Commission? and (3) What is the nature of the Great Commission?

The dispensational understanding of the Great Commission, as indicated in the response to the three questions above, may be designated the Pietistic Model. By that I mean that dispensationalism seeks personal piety, while denying the possibility and even desirability of cultural conversion.

The amillennialist and historic premillennialist views may be termed the Composite Model. By that I mean that although they do encourage Christian cultural engagement, nevertheless, their systems allow only sporadic, temporary, partial victories for Christianity in terms of any beneficent cultural influence.

The postmillennial understanding of the Great Commission may be designated the Transformational Model. It not only seeks but *expects* both widespread personal piety and Christian cultural transformation.

Again, all non-postmillennial views deny widespread and enduring gospel success in transforming men, nations, and cultures in this age. Let me illustrate this by a few citations.

This same pessimism regarding the gospel's success is evident among historic premillennialists, such as George E. Ladd:

---

23. H. de Jongste and J. M. van Krimpen, *The Bile and the Life of the Christian* (Philadelphia: Presbyterian and Reformed, 1968), p. 27.

24. John F. Walvoord, Review of Donald Guthrie, *The Relevance of John's Apocalypse* in *Bibliotheca Sacra* 147:586 (April-June, 1990) 251.

"the gospel is not to conquer the world and subdue all nations to itself. Hatred, conflict, and war will continue to characterize the age until the coming of the Son of Man."[25]

Such a view obviously is held by amillennialists, as indicated by Louis Berkhof: "The fundamental idea . . . that the whole world will gradually be won for Christ, . . . is not in harmony with the picture of the end of the ages found in Scripture. The Bible . . . does not lead us to expect the conversion of the world."[26] But dispensational writings are the most widely read and evidence the most vigorous opposition to the cultural influence of the gospel, hence my special attention to their views.

Given the widespread popularity of the dispensational system among evangelicals and dispensationalism's attempted disavowal of historical pessimism,[27] I will cite several of their writings in order to press the point home most convincingly. Dispensationalist Charles Stevens puts it about as clearly as can be, when he states: "The New Testament concept of the church in this age is typified by the wilderness tabernacle, serving a pilgrim people, built with traveling facilities, 'going' after the lost, visiting, seeking, praying."[28] John Walvoord writes: "It is not God's plan and purpose to bring righteousness and peace to the earth in this present age. We will never attain the postmillennial dream of peace on earth through the influence of the church."[29] Wayne House and Thomas Ice agree: "Nowhere in the New Testament does it teach the agenda of Christianizing the institutions of the world."[30]

Dave Hunt follows suit in downplaying postmillennial expectations: "this impossible goal of Christianizing the world is now

25. Ladd, *Theology*, p. 202.

26. Louis Berkhof, *Systematic Theology* (Grand Rapids: Wm. B. Eerdmans, 1941), p. 718.

27. See: House and Ice, *Dominion Theology*, "Does Premillennialism Believe in Dominion in History?" (pp. 142-150).

28. Charles H. Stevens, in Charles Lee Feinberg, ed., *Prophecy and the Seventies* (Chicago: Moody, 1970), p. 110.

29. John F. Walvoord, in Charles Lee Feinberg, ed., *Prophecy and the Seventies* (Chicago: Moody, 1971), p. 211.

30. H. Wayne House and Thomas D. Ice, *Dominion Theology: Blessing or Curse?* (Portland, OR: Multnomah, 1988), p. 155.

being presented as the long overlooked true intent of the Great Commission."[31] Elsewhere he writes: "It is a further 'reduction of Christianity' to suggest that the Great Commission calls us to reassert the allegedly lost 'dominion' over this earth and its lower creatures. And it is a gross perversion to turn the Great Commission into a 'cultural mandate' which assigns to the church the task of taking over the world to establish the Kingdom of God before Christ returns."[32]

Hal Lindsey vigorously denies what the premise of this present book demonstrates: "There is absolutely nothing, stated or implied, to support the Dominionist[33] interpretation of the Great Commission in either Mark, Luke, or Acts. The purpose of the decision demanded is forgiveness of sin and a spiritual new birth, not the reformation of society . . . ."[34] Fundamentalist George Dollar notes of dispensationalist fundamentalists that they believe "the whole world scene is one of deterioration and will so continue till the rapture takes place, and that our main business should be to rescue people out of the mess and not try to improve it or preserve its good characteristics."[35]

Conclusion

As I have engaged the text of the Great Commission in resolution of the questions before us, I have cited and interacted with various writers from among the various pessimistic and pietistic schools of thought. I did not do this with a view to demeaning evangelical brethren, but in order to demonstrate by documentary evidence the radical differences among evangelicals regarding the Great Commission. In addition, I hope

---

31. Hunt, *Whatever Happened?*, p. 178.

32. Dave Hunt, *CIB Bulletin* (Camarillo, CA: Christian Information Bulletin), May, 1988, p. 1.

33. "Dominionist" is a term employed by some to describe those Christians who seek Christian cultural renewal by the application of biblical principles, thus seeking the visible exercise of Christ's "dominion from sea to sea" (Zech. 9:10; cp. Eph. 1:21; 1 Pet. 4:11; Rev. 1:6). Adherents of Dominion Theology or Christian Reconstructionism long for the day when Christianity becomes "dominant" in the world of human affairs.

34. Lindsey, *Holocaust*, p. 275.

35. George Dollar, *A History of Fundamentalism in America* (Greenville, SC: Bob Jones University Press, 1973), p. 278.

the reader has seen the overwhelming Scriptural support for the postmillennial view of the Great Commission, which has recently begun to be assaulted as "a road to holocaust" (because it has no place for the political exaltation of the nation of Israel over other nations) and "this worldly" (because it is concerned with life in the tangible world, as well as in heaven).[36]

The dispensationalist is alarmed at the very thought of Christian cultural transformation. In his view to attempt such "is to err so grievously as to lead one into a program that is hopeless; it calls necessarily for the adopting of means that are unauthorized, and the setting of a goal that is unattainable as it is unscriptural. Herein lies the great mistake of the 'kingdom builders' (their tribe decreases) who have as their goal a vision of Christianizing the world."[37] In opposition to the view presented herein, the dispensationalist retorts: "Although [postmillennialists] see evangelism as part of the Great Commission, their main focus and goal is to Christianize the world's culture and political systems, and to take dominion over them. This is not even what God had in mind in the Eden Mandate, but it is certainly not what the Great Commission teaches."[38]

Due especially to dispensationalism's systemic requirements (teaching the God-ordained ineffectiveness and decline of the Church in history[39]), that system of theology inadvertently waters down the command:

Go therefore and make disciples of all the nations, baptizing them in the name of the Father and of the Son and of the Holy Spirit, teaching them to observe all things that I have commanded you. (Matthew 28:19-20a).

36. Lindsey, *Road to Holocaust* and Hunt, *Whatever Happened to Heaven?*, *passim*.
37. C. H. Stevens in *Prophecy and the Seventies*, p. 101.
38. Lindsey, *Holocaust*, p. 273. His reference to the Edenic Mandate in Genesis 1:26-28 represents a contradiction in another of his writings: "At the time of his creation man was given legal authority to rule himself and all of the earth.' Hal Lindsey, *Satan is Alive and Well on Planet Earth* (Grand Rapids: Zondervan, 1972), p. 56.
39. See pp. 148-151. "This current world is headed toward judgment. . . . [T]he message and activities for believers should be, 'Flee the wrath to come by finding safety in Jesus Christ.'" House and Ice, *Dominion Theology*, p. 356.

CONCLUSION

CONCLUSION

"Hallowed by Thy name. Thy kingdom come. Thy will be done, On earth as it is in heaven. . . . For Thine is the kingdom, and the power, and the glory, forever. Amen" (Matt. 6:9-10, 13b).

I now have completed a fairly thorough analysis of the Great Commission. Hopefully I have provided solid, Bible-based answers to our three opening questions:

What is the Great Commission?
What is the goal of the Great Commission?
What is the nature of the Great Commission?

I trust that the answers provided will be hope inducing, vision expanding, and labor encouraging.

It seems to me that the change that is most needful today in Christian circles in order to recover the greatness of the Great Commission is a major shift in practical, applied Christianity. The contemporary Church is afflicted by three corrosive agents:

(1) Rampant smiley-faced superficiality, so characteristic of mega-ministries and much of Christian publishing and broadcasting, which largely is resultant from inattention to the Great Commission.

(2) Decades old cultural retreatism, which largely has been engendered by a misconception of the Great Commission.

(3) The time perspective problem, which largely involves a denial of the Great Commission time perspective.

The Church and Superficiality

Regarding the matter of superficiality, John A. Sproule laments: "The tragedy today . . . is the apparent disinterest in the preaching of doctrine in the church. . . . Caught up in the craze for 'Christian' entertainment and psychology, the church is worse off for it."[1] Regarding the accelerating changes in this direction inside American evangelical churches, David Wells warns that "the impetus to change is coming from *without* rather than from within, and this impetus is primarily sociological, not theological."[2]

Too much in the popular church growth mentality reduces the role of sound biblical preaching and teaching in deference to crowd-pleasing antics to draw the play-oriented masses into churches.[3] These masses must then continually be entertained by throwing Christian theology to the lions. Of last century's

---

1. John A. Sproule in John S. Feinberg, ed., *Continuity and Discontinuity: Perspectives on the Relationship Between the Old and New Testament* (Westchester, IL: Crossway Books, 1988), p. 318. James Davison Hunter has written a powerful critique of the theological drift in evangelicalism entitled: *Evangelicalism: The Coming Generation* (University of Chicago Press, 1987). In an article on Hunter's book, entitled "Theological Drift: Christian Higher Ed the Culprit?," Randy Frame notes: "Hunter argued in the book that contemporary evangelicalism is moving away from tenets of belief and practice long considered orthodox. There are some who say that the current conflict at Grace Theological Seminary exemplifies Hunter's observations. . . ." (*Christianity Today*, April, 9, 1990, p. 43). See article in the same issue: "Trouble at Grace: Making Waves or Guarding the Truth?," p. 46.

2. David Wells, "Assaulted by Modernity," *Christianity Today* 34:3 (February 19, 1990) 16. A remarkable illustration of this may be found in the conservative Presbyterian Church in America's *The PCA Messenger*. A reader, Carl Gauger, complained in a letter to the editor: "I find in the article . . . further confirmation of a disturbing trend in evangelicalism. Although we continue to voice confidence in the inerrancy of the Bible, we are tending to use it less and less. . . . In this article . . . *we are given no pretense to believe [the writer's assumptions] because of any biblical authority*. It is disappointing enough to see psychology parading in a cloak of misquoted biblical references, but when even the pretense of Biblical authority is removed, I think God's people should rise up and cry foul." Editor Bob Sweet responded (in part): "But do you examine everything you read so critically? Do you require 'biblical authority' for everything?" (pp. 3, 4). Wells' "impetus to change" is often from secular psychological theories.

3. See Richard Quebedeaux, *By What Authority: The Rise of Personality Cults in American Christianity* (San Francisco: Harper and Row, 1982). For important correctives to this work, see: Michael R. Gilstrap's review, "Media Theo-Pop" in James B. Jordan, ed., *The Failure of the American Baptist Culture*, vol 1 of *Christianity and Civilization* (Tyler, TX: Geneva Divinity School, 1982), pp. 99-110.

ınfluential evangelist, Dwight L. Moody, Weisberger writes: he "completed the reduction of evangelism to a matter of technique and personality."⁴ North's comments are *apropos*:

> Is it any wonder that the doctrine of eternal damnation is de-empha-sized in preaching today? Is it any wonder that God is spoken of mostly as a God of love, and seldom as the God of indescribable eternal wrath? D. L. Moody, the turn-of-the-century American evan-gelist, set the pattern by refusing to preach about hell. He made the preposterous statement that "Terror never brought a man in yet." That a major evangelist could make such a theologically unsupported statement and expect anyone to take him seriously testifies to the theologically debased state of modern evangelicalism. It has gotten no better since he said it.⁵

If there is no sound doctrinal base to the Christian life, there can be no proper starting point for a holistic Christian faith.

The Church and Retreatism

Regarding the matter of retreatism, Francis A. Schaeffer has written:

> The basic problem of the Christians in this country in the last eighty years or so, in regard to society and in regard to government, is that they have seen things in bits and pieces instead of totals. . . .
> Why have the Christians been so slow to understand . . . ? [It is traceable to] a deficient, "platonic" spirituality. It [is] platonic in the sense that Pietism made a sharp division between the "spiritual" and the "material" world — giving little, or no, importance to the "materi-al" world. . . .
> Christianity and spirituality were shut up to a small, isolated part of life.⁶

4. Bernard Wisberger, *They Gathered at the River* (Boston: Little, Brown, 1958), p. 177. For the problems created by Moody's revivalism, see: George Dollar, *A History of Funda-mentalism in America* (Greenville, SC: Bob Jones University, 1973), ch. 5, "New Winds Blowing."
5. Gary North, *Tools of Dominion: The Case Laws of Exodus* (Tyler, TX: Institute for Christian Economics, 1990), p. 167. North got this quote from Stanley N. Gundry, who was cited by George M. Marsden. He then comments: "Perhaps someone will cite me, making it three-stage faith in footnotes" (p. 167, n. 126). Consider it done!
6. Francis A. Schaeffer, *A Christian Manifesto* (Westchester, IL: Crossway Books, 1981),

Having isolated life into neat compartments and having exalt-ed the "spiritual" over the "material," the Church has given up on the world and retreated into its own four walls. The very fact that churches often sponsor "retreats" inadvertently demon-strates the acceptability of this mentality. *When there is a tendency to retreatism, there is no proper practice of a holistic Christian faith.*

There is dangerous atrophy in the Body of Christ (the Church) due to chronic retreatism and the more recent onset of acute superficiality. And the recovery of the true strength of the family, the Church, and the State will take both effort and time. Fortunately, the Great Commission, when properly understood, provides us with the strength needed for the effort ("I am with you," promises the One with "all authority") and the time neces-sary to the task ("even to the end of the age").

The Church and Time

Few things have been more destructive to the implementation of a well-rounded, biblically-grounded Christian worldview than one's time perspective. A classic, though inadvertent illustration of this, is available in an interview with evangelist Billy Graham a few years back:

> Q. If you had to live your life over again, what would you do differ-ently?
>
> A. One of my great regrets is that I have not studied enough. I wish I had studied more and preached less. . . . Donald Barnhouse said that if he knew the Lord was coming in three years he would spend two of them studying and one preaching. I'm trying to make it up.[7]

A similar problem is admitted by Tim LaHaye. Many Chris-tians are committed to the approaching end of the age, with all of its horror (according to their dispensational view):

---

pp. 17, 18, 19. See also: Franky Schaeffer, *Addicted to Mediocrity: 20th Century Christians and the Arts* (Westchester, IL: Crossway Books, 1981); Gary North, ed., *Biblical Blueprint Series* (Ft. Worth, TX: Dominion Press, 1986-1987), ten volumes.

7. "Taking the World's Temperature" (no author) in *Christianity Today* (Sept. 23, 1977), p. 19

Most knowledgeable Christians are looking for the Second Coming of Christ and the tribulation period that He predicted would come before the end of the age. Because present world conditions are so similar to those the Bible prophesies for the last days. . . , they conclude that a takeover of our culture by the forces of evil is inevitable; so they do nothing to resist it.[8]

Much of the modern spread of this foreshortened time perspective is traceable to the Brethren movement in the 1830s. W. Blair Neatby gives an interesting analysis of the Brethren devotion to such:

Brethrenism is the child of the study of unfulfilled prophecy and of the expectation of the immediate return of the Saviour. If any one had told the first Brethren that three quarters of a century might elapse and the Church still be on earth, the answer would probably have been a smile, partly of pity, partly of disapproval, wholly of incredulity. Yet so it has proved. It is impossible not to respect hopes so congenial to ardent devotion; yet it is clear now that Brethrenism took shape under the influence of a delusion, and that delusion left its traces, more or less deeply, on the most distinctive features of the system.[9]

Billy Graham, Tim LaHaye, and millions of other Christians hold to the "any-moment" view of the Coming of Christ, which shortens their historical perspective. Some have carried this view to logical, but embarrassing, extremes. We see the clearest examples in Edgar C. Whisenant's *88 Reasons Why the Rapture Is in 1988*[10] and Hal Lindsey's *The 1980s: Countdown to Armageddon*.[11] Soon to join them is Richard Rhuling, M.D., with his

---

8. Tim LaHaye, *The Battle for the Mind* (Old Tappen, NJ: Revell, 1980), p. 217.

9. W. Blair Neatby, *A History of the Plymouth Brethren*, p. 339. Cited from Joseph M. Canfield, "Discussion Paper No. 3: The Delusion of Imminence!" (unpublished manuscript, June 30, 1988), p. 1.

10. Edgar C. Whisenant, *88 Reasons Why the Rapture Is in 1988* (Nashville, TN: World Bible Society, 1988). Whisenant claims to have published several million copies of this work. After his initial failure (the Rapture did not occur in September, 1988, as he predicted), he even tried to update it to January, 1989, then September, 1989. He soon lost his following.

11. Hal Lindsey, *The 1980s: Countdown to Armageddon* (New York: Bantam, 1980). Though Lindsey is not as bold, his sensational books lead in the same direction, with such statements as: *"The decade of the 1980's could very well be the last decade of history as we know*

new book *Sword Over America*, that is said to point to the early 1990s as the time for the Battle of Armageddon.[12]

It is sad to say, but these men are following in a long train failed prophets.[13] This "any moment" viewpoint kept Graham diligently working, even if not carefully preparing for the long haul. This has kept too many other Christians sitting back, away from the fray (except for a few notable areas of exception, such as anti-pornography and pro-life advocacy), while expecting the end. But a long, developmental, hope-filled view of history is fundamental to any serious Bible-based approach to the whole of life.[14] *If there is a tendency to promote a "blocked future," there will be no promotion of a holistic Christian faith.*

Conclusion

A proper understanding of the Great Commission will be essential for the Church to collect itself in preparation for the 1990s and the challenges of the looming new century. Even though we are hearing many reports of "the staggering growth of the church in previously non-Christian parts of the world" and that "in all of Asia and most of Africa, unprecedented numbers are coming to Christ,"[15] for which we are thankful, we must not become lax in our promotion of sound doctrine and practice. A recent report showed that such popular evangelical theologians as J. N. D. Anderson, Clark Pinnock, and Charles Kraft, allow that "if any unevangelized person repents and desires God's mercy, he will be saved by the work of Christ even

---

it" (p. 8, emphasis his).

12. See: Jim Ashley, "Ruhling Believes 'Crisis' Events Near," *Chattanooga News-Free Press*, October 7, 1989, Church News Section.

13. See: Dwight Wilson, *Armageddon Now! The Premillenarian Response to Russia and Israel Since 1917* (Grand Rapids, MI: Baker, 1977).

14. "Christianity is a force for total transformation, even of the cosmos (Rom. 8:18-22). Nevertheless, it is not self-consciously revolutionary. It does not seek to overthrow civil governments by elitist-imposed force. Instead, it steadily overthrows all governments — personal, familistic, church, and civil — by the cumulative spread of the gospel and the process of *institutional replacement*. This is the New Testament kingdom principle of leaven (Matt. 13:33)." North, *Tools of Dominion*, p. 189. This, obviously, is a program that requires much time.

15. Terry C. Muck, "Many Mansions?" in *Christianity Today* 34:8 (May 14, 1990) 14.

though ignorant of that work."[16] It noted further that such noteworthy evangelicals as J. I. Packer and Roger Nicole "allow some possibility for the salvation of the unevangelized," while Donald Bloesch "affirms the possibility of conversion after death."[17]

Christians must begin applying the Great Commission, indeed, *all* of Scripture, to the fundamental institutions of social order: the family, the Church, and the State. This will be especially incumbent upon American Christians, who are now not only facing a secular humanistic government on one hand, but also an increasingly non-Christian society on the other. "There are now more Muslims than Methodists in the U. S."[18] In fact, there has been a 300% increase in the Muslim population in just ten years.[19]

Regarding the family, we must remember that if we "train up a child in the way he should go" then "even when he is old he will not depart from it" (Prov. 22:6).

Regarding the Church, we must recall that "It is time for judgment to begin with the household of God" (1 Pet. 4:17a).

Regarding the State, we must recognize that "If My people who are called by My name humble themselves and pray, and seek My face and turn from their wicked ways, then I will hear from heaven, will forgive their sin, and will heal their land" (2 Chron. 7:14).

In all of this we must bow before Him Who has "all authority in heaven and on earth." We do so by obeying His commands to "go therefore and make disciples of all the nations, baptizing them in the name of the Father and the Son and the Holy Spirit, teaching them to observe all that I commanded you." In so doing we may always rejoice in the confident hope "lo, I am with you always, even to the end of the age." And as we engage

---

16. John Sanders, "The Perennial Debate" in *Christianity Today* 34:8 (May 14, 1990) 21. This article deals with "the question of salvation for those who have never heard of Christ" (p. 21).

17. *Ibid.*

18. Colin Chapman, "The Riddle of Religions," in *Christianity Today*, 34:8 (May 14, 1990) 16.

19. *Ibid.*, p. 19.

the task we may confidently declare "Amen" (Heb. "so be it"). For this is *the greatness of the Great Commission* found in Matthew 28:18-20.

SCRIPTURE INDEX

INDEX